SPIRITUAL
LEADERSHIP

The Quest for Integrity

LEONARD DOOHAN

Paulist Press
New York/Mahwah, NJ

Cover design by Joy Taylor
Book design by Lynn Else

Library of Congress Cataloging-in-Publication Data

Doohan, Leonard,
    Spiritual leadership : the quest for integrity / Leonard Doohan.
        p.   cm.
    Includes bibliographical references.
    ISBN 978-0-8091-4495-2 (alk. paper)
    1. Leadership—Religious aspects—Christianity, I. Title.
BV4597.53.L43D66 2007
253—dc22

                                                        2007020985

Published by Paulist Press
997 Macarthur Boulevard
Mahwah, New Jersey 07430

www.paulistpress.com

Printed and bound in the
United States of America

CONTENTS

Dedication

For my wife Helen with all my love

INTRODUCTION

When I think of a spiritual leader I think of a person with tremendous energy, who knows what life is about and is living it well, who is comfortable with chosen values and lives them with integrity, who knows the value of other people and cherishes their lives and input, and who is both rooted in the historical values of a chosen tradition and yet is convinced that any tradition must change to be equally relevant in the future as it was in the past. Above all, a spiritual leader is motivated by an experience that has touched him or her profoundly and has influenced the way he or she now lives. This kind of person shows no embarrassment in talking about the experience, and makes decisions based on the values of this experience.

This faith-motivated commitment is desperately needed today, especially when we see so many organizations full of leaders with the wrong mind-set. This experience that changes a person's life is what we call an experience of "faith." When we talk about "spiritual leadership," we refer to leadership motivated and inspired by the spiritual values of a person's "faith." So, spiritual leadership is a leadership that is motivated by everything that one holds dear in the depths of his or her own heart as the result of a personal experience that has changed one's life and way of living it in the future. This is not the fruits of a workshop, nor of the acquisition of new skills, nor even of a new experience. Rather it is a call felt deep within one's heart. This personal experience could be the result of an experience of love, or of suffering, or of another's concern, or of reflection into a world tragedy, or of insights gained in a religious tradition. Thus, Greenleaf was not only motivated by his Quaker tradition but gives special mention to the impact of personally experiencing the story of Leo in Hermann Hesse's "Journey to the East."[1] The businessman,

Steven Camden, found his life totally changed forever by the experience he gained in encounter with Maria in the story narrated by Bolman and Deal.[2] The nine leaders terminated in a time of downsizing in Mary Pulley's book found in their own emptiness a new power within themselves for future growth.[3] In each case the experience resulted in changing one's life—all of it, both spiritual and material. I am convinced that spiritual leadership produces this reintegration of all aspects of life.[4]

Spiritual leadership is a form of leadership that results from integrity, living every aspect of leadership based on the core motivating values. Spiritual leadership is not something you add on to an already existing leadership style; rather it permeates everything that one does, whether at home, in social life, or at work. The best leaders are the ones who are grounded in motivating values and have "faith," and they live differently as a result of it. They believe in themselves for sure, but also in values beyond themselves. You cannot pick and choose values or virtues; either they motivate you from within in all you do, or they do not. Sprinkling your leadership with assorted virtues from a variety of sources is simply a leadership technique to make one's management style more palatable—to others or to oneself. Even the components of transformational leadership can be implemented as technique.

When one lives spiritual leadership, that person does not only become more spiritual; rather he or she becomes integrally human. This splendid task of becoming who we are capable of being means journeying into the depths of oneself, stretching out to make one's own those values that in a special experience became the motivation of life. This experience may be called a conversion, a breakthrough, enlightenment, or a fundamental option. Greenleaf even spoke about "a dream deferred."[5] The sun is setting on many leadership styles that may have been effective in the past, and already we are seeing pockets of spiritual leadership in a sea of mediocrity, leadership that is based on inner convictions—principle-centered leadership. The term *spiritual leadership* refers to a leadership that is the result of living with integrity those values that are the basis of one's life, and making all decisions in light of those values. There can never be a separation between life values and leadership practice.

In recent years, we have witnessed many individuals who truly want to lead others as a service to the community, and we have also seen some individual and corporate disasters in failed leadership, whether in business, politics, or religion, that have cried out for the healing and correction that come with a clearer understanding of leadership and with a rededication to this vocation. Furthermore, Christian men and women increasingly yearn to be models of the Christian values of leadership in every aspect of their lives—professional, family, community, and societal. Jesus spoke explicitly of the kind of leadership he expected from his followers and also identified certain kinds of leadership that he found unacceptable in his followers. This book is a challenge to laymen and laywomen—but equally to lay ministers, religious, and clergy, to become inspired by the values of Christian leadership. Our world today needs leaders like never before, but leaders who are guided by the principle-centered values of Christianity.

People's commitment to leadership development in recent years focuses on four reactions. Some have sought greater information to enlarge their knowledge base, and this is foundational. Some have benefited from workshops that provide new skills. Others have participated in programs, courses, and workshops that have given them new experiences of what leading others could look like. Still others have made the inward journey to discover self-identity, and this has made them more aware than ever of their own responsibility, vocation, and destiny in the world of leadership.

This book focuses on the fourth point, urging readers to discover their own call to leadership and to appreciate their own responsibility and destiny in the service of others. It seeks to identify trends in the last couple of decades that led to the current focus on the leader's inner self. It emphasizes the integral nature of leadership—that it touches every facet of one's personality. It insists on the fact that leadership is part of who one is, and not just what one does. It concludes that leadership today is spiritual leadership, part of one's integral human maturing.

In recent decades there has been an increasing appreciation of spiritual leadership as the leadership that will assure honesty, integrity, the common good, and both individual and communal growth. A variety of authors have focused their call for spiritual leadership on one dimension or another that seems to serve as the focal point for their contribution to spiritual leadership and that also became in each case the title of a book. Thus, Robert Greenleaf (1977) spoke of "servant leadership," Stephen Covey (1991) "principle-centered leadership," J. M. Kouzes and B. Z. Posner (1993) "credibility," LaRue Hosmer (1994) "moral leadership." Others like Nancy Eggert (1998) spoke of "contemplative leadership," Donna Markham (1999) "spiritlinking leadership," Barbara Maskoff and Gary Wenet (2000) "the inner work of leaders," Robert Spitzer (2000) "the spirit of leadership," and Russ Moxley (2000) "leadership and spirit." Along the same lines Genie Laborde (1987) described leadership as "influencing with integrity," Joseph Badaracco (1989) as "a quest for integrity," Jay Conger (1994) as "discovering spirituality in leadership," Jack Hawley (1993) as "reawakening the Spirit," Terrence Deal and Lee Bolman (1995) as "leading with soul," Dorothy Marcic (1997) as "managing with the wisdom of love," and Gilbert Fairholm (2001) as "mastering inner leadership." All these authors speak about spiritual leadership, each one focusing their insights on a critical facet of spiritual leadership.

This book is written for those individuals who want to integrate their leadership with the values of their lives. It presumes that readers have or search for the integration of the values of faith and the effectiveness of leadership. It is written from a Christian perspective, even though it can just as easily be applied and used by readers with a different faith experience. The book asks the reader to pause and to examine if his or her leadership is the best it can be, whether one's leadership qualities in work enhance one's personal life, and whether the Christian values that one accepted in baptism lead to a different style of leadership.

So the book is an invitation to think about oneself and the kind of leader one wishes to be and to become. Leadership is a total way of life, a way of living our humanity, a form of implementing one's philosophy of life, a way of looking at one's self-identity and destiny. There are several chapters that are developmental and sequential, moving from a confrontation of today's problems, to an appreciation of common trends, to a focus on spiritual leadership. Further chapters focus on components of spiritual leadership, and the book concludes with an invitation to dedicate oneself to spiritual leadership. However, each of these chapters is written in a way that readers can choose one or another out of sequence to simply reflect on an individual aspect that is important at a particular time.

Today's world and its many manifestations in organizational life are crying out for a new dedication to the vocation of leadership. The greedy, the abusers, the power hungry, the selfish will always be with us. May there always be those men and women who will give their lives to leadership in service for others. May dedicated Christians exemplify a Christian style of leadership, confident that the world yearns for such values.

1

THE DANGEROUS POSSIBILITY OF TAKING LEADERSHIP SERIOUSLY

1. Has the Recent Emphasis on Leadership Got Us Anywhere?

Leadership has become a major issue in all forms of organizations—business, health care, military, and religious. Training programs focus on preparing leaders, and increasingly people want to know that their bosses are truly effective leaders. "Leadership" is one of the key buzzwords of the last twenty years, and individual books and entire series dedicated to this topic have increased beyond most people's expectations. Different authors have focused on what they see as the major issue that makes leadership work and have stressed every imaginable key concept from vision to creativity, or strategic action to courage, or credibility to TQM (total quality management). We have been bombarded with techniques, strategies, and insights on visioning, team building, collaboration, negotiation, leading cross-functional teams, managing corporate culture, and empowerment. Still, we find few great leaders or model organizations. Some responses are strikingly different from each other, and many authors still address the topic as if they are presuming a top manager will grow into becoming a great leader, and thus the business will flourish. Some studies interview top CEOs and presidents to identify the best components of leadership, presuming top managers would be the best source for such views. Perhaps this is because the often-communicated impression is that the best of management with its planning, administration,

1

and oversight merges into leadership, as individuals learn some of the endless list of new skills.

Nowadays, we have a "new workplace," "new management," "new skills," and "a new paradigm." We have "seven spiritual laws of success," "seven pathways to mastery," "seven skills of highly effective leaders," "eight universal laws of leadership," the "nine natural laws of leadership," "seven zones for leadership," and so on. One writer having browsed through the many books published on the topic of leadership concludes "they all propose radically new, dynamic roles….Everyone is talking about how leadership has changed."[1] Moreover, changes are now a permanent feature of a leader's role—there will be no period of calm after this storm. The understanding of leadership and our expectations of leaders have permanently changed, and the change is so great that both writers and practitioners refer to a paradigm shift, a transformation, an awakening, and others simply speak of "the new leadership."

In spite of all the recent emphasis on leadership I, and I am sure many readers, can honestly say that we have met very few good leaders and many mediocre ones who have neither the vision nor the courage to do what needs to be done. In fact, if many workers had the opportunity of choosing to pay for the central administration of their organization, they probably would not, since they do not believe their administration is worth it. Furthermore, spending time with today's so-called leaders can seriously impair one's own ability to ever lead others.[2] Bennis, who has given many insights into leadership, concludes, "Ironically, probably more has been written and less is known about leadership than about any other topic in the behavioral sciences."[3] There has been so much hope for leadership development but it has been so little justified; it is disheartening to look at our so-called leaders today. Bryman concludes, "the results produced by the study of leadership have been a major disappointment for many of us working within organizational behavior."[4] Some describe leadership as "the search for excellence," but so much emphasis on excellence suggests mediocrity must be everywhere. In times of change and uncertainty like ours, we might be tempted to say with Juvenal (VI, 347), "Put the bars on the windows and watch out. But who will guard us against those who stand watch over us?"

2. Failed Organizations

Many contemporary organizations are still overmanaged and underled. Given recent developments in leadership studies, they could all be so different, as scholars have redefined what it means to be a living and life-giving organization—components of which we will see later. Some charismatic individuals have transformed their organizations, so that workers cannot even remember what theirs used to be like. But such changed structures are few, and it is more common to find that yesterday's giants are today's dinosaurs. How many organizations do you know where the followers are better informed and more skilled than their managers? Is it not common to still find the power of hierarchical status with its temptations to manipulate others and situations and to use power to push others to burnout, to control others by lack of information, to refuse opportunity for input into decision making?[5] Some managers hold on because they are fearful, frozen by their own inability to move or to change—this happens in every organization. These managers, skilled at things that used to work, cling to the known past, anxious and afraid of all change. "The journey to the future is guarded by a thousand [such] people [self-]appointed to protect the past."[6] Some managers, even some who are quite young, hold on until retirement because they want their privilege and exaggerated salaries to continue for just a few more years before the inevitable changes come. These managers then turn to superficialities that can guarantee they keep going, along with their salaries, until retirement, at which time others can do what they like. Some managers hold on because of their dedication to the organization's mission which they arrogantly believe they alone know and appreciate. Such individuals generate myths about their own authority, while constantly mimicking the worst practices of the corporate world. Some managers hold on because they enjoy the power their position gives them. The resulting situation led a professor at Harvard Business School to claim, "Business in America has lost its way, adrift in a sea of managerial mediocrity, desperately needing leadership to face worldwide economic competition."[7]

Organizations that promise health often deliver societal sickness, those that promise care often deliver control, those that promise service often deliver authority, and those that promise salvation often deliver dependent guilt and enslavement. Nowadays, 55 percent of organizational changes fail, and all the suffering the changes caused were for no purpose.[8] We are currently in a period of downsizing—an activity undertaken by inexperienced managers to persuade themselves that they are doing something. Yet, 66 percent of such efforts led to no increased productivity, 55 percent led to no financial gains, and 80 percent of the affected companies experienced low employee morale.[9] We live in technological times in which we have lost the personal attention to others we used to have, paperless societies in which the proliferation of paperwork has increased by 51 percent, and homes with computerized phone systems where an individual can be kept waiting for over half an hour before listening to a recorded voice. Today's thoughtless organizations are managed by individuals without leadership, and the organization itself suffers from "organizational disabilities," among which is the collective resistance to learn and change.[10] Koestenbaum suggests, "The average organization is in some sort of pain. It varies from restlessness, uncertainty, and floating anxiety to severe despair. The pain, in its pure form, is not treatable."[11]

Much of the pain results directly from a lack of leadership in the organizations we serve. One writer who has extensively studied the diminished commitment found in many organizations today says, "Too many organizations have needlessly alienated their key resource—their employees. With downsizing, cost-cutting, mergers, and other changes, employees have been given the distinct feeling that they are simply costs to be trimmed. Those who are left are told to work harder to keep their jobs. They are asked to sacrifice and give up benefits. This atmosphere does not exactly inspire high morale, or a willingness to take responsibility."[12] Amidst this large societal despair, our leaders and our organizations are failing us, and employees all over the place are withdrawing their commitment and allegiance from undeserving organizations and unworthy leaders. Dedicated workers always give some commitment simply because they have pride in being professional, but there is an additional level of discretionary commitment that workers can withdraw when their connection to an organization is weakened. Such organizations lose the energy, enthusiasm, and dedication of their people, as shortsighted managers kill the service, innovation, quality, imagination, and creative spark of their major resource. In the future, we will need to change the parameters of what followers will stand for and what they will not.

Decisions that negatively impact dedicated workers almost always imply a lack of managerial planning. One insightful professor felt his task was to "teach students to protect themselves from pervasive 'organizational abuse.'"[13] A glance at any week's newspapers or news programs shows how right he was. Bosses who claim they can make "those tough decisions" are frequently visionless individuals scrambling to regain the organizational influence they ought to have had all along. The problem is that the systematic approaches that are often used are not getting us where we want to be. We must change the way organizations lead, change their culture and systems. Although we need leaders, today's organizations often make it difficult for individuals to lead the organization in ways different "than we've always done it," thus preserving themselves and protecting themselves against the needed change.

Workers today are frequently more knowledgeable about their organization than are their bosses. They often appreciate that we must face almost total instability in the years ahead. But these people can respond to almost any challenge provided they are given support and the leadership they need to use their talents effectively. Unfortunately as managers face more difficult challenges they easily become more autocratic, making decisions in private as if they alone knew what they were doing. The neglect of the input of others in times of crises is a very serious mistake.

Most organizations today, when they appoint managers or leaders, rarely ask if the appointee can manage or lead. Some turn out to be micro managers unable to see people and their visions and needs because of their emphasis on the petty accomplishments of their small-screen focus. Some organizational professionals are managerial nomads, wandering from one job to another as soon as they accomplish some picayune issue that readies their resume for the next step on the ladder of success.

I can think of only a few organizations of which their managers or leaders could be proud—organizations that encourage the vision, communication, empowerment, and trust that can foster a changing organizational culture. These organizations offer a compelling vision for which all workers can strive, they develop and earn commitment to the new vision, and they can institutionalize the vision. They are open to change and constantly fight off efforts of the fearful to domesticate and control the creativity frequently found in the hearts of an organization's employees.

3. Frustrated Hope in Leaders

"People want their company and its leaders to show them respect, to treat them with dignity, to offer them jobs with meaning, to let them know what is going on, to invite them into decision making, and to offer them opportunities to control their work."[14] It goes without saying that these practices do not cost anything. Yet, how many organizations do you know where these practices are valued? Is it not rather a common experience that many managers and potential leaders make unhealthy choices for power and control? Is it not true that they underappreciate their employees, leaving many talented individuals out of developments, doomed to a working life at the margins? Some of the greatest stress that people experience today comes from the frustrated hope in our leaders.

Some pseudoleaders do much damage to their organizations not only by thwarting their growth but by creating unhealthy working environments that either draw the worst out of people or leave them depressed and sick at their own inability to get out of the situation that is stunting their values and growth. In fact one author bluntly states, "Leaders are often villains, and…it is very difficult to be an effective leader and at the same time a good person." The author goes on to suggest that leadership "has no place for those practicing nothing but the right and the good."[15] Such an approach produces *arrogant autocrats* who ignore others, suppress their ideas, and intimidate when challenged. One author concludes, "These are the leaders who approach ventures with a sureness of self based on their own pathology rather than on their command of information or clarity of insight."[16] Such leaders have a deep suspicion of liberty—others', not their own!

Other managers and potential leaders are not quite so blunt and give the impression of welcoming participation, but they are *failed facilitators.* Empowerment cannot be taught by people who have practiced disempowerment for years, and workers quickly see through insincerity. "No amount of rhetoric can tune out the intense decibels of managerial hypocrisy or double standards. To be real, to be lasting, change must be genuine and must spring from the deepest, most basic levels of human needs and values."[17] Some self-styled leaders fail to show the consistent commitment that being a facilitator implies. At times they are too optimistic, then too cautious to get anything done, too combative even when unnecessary, and then too unfocused and so they backslide. Unfortunately, the failed facilitator is often a good talker and seems to have the talents necessary for the work at hand. However, it is all show and talk and no substance. In fact, this pseudoleader is threatened by any pressure to do something either personally or collaboratively.

Some administrators make so many mistakes they seem to have a natural ability for it. Typical indicators of incompetent administration include useless restructuring, a myopic immersion in trivial data, and the constant development of strategic plans that enthuse no one. These *blind visionaries,* who surrender to mediocrity in their work and indifference toward their employees, may well occupy important positions, but careful observation quickly shows that little actual management is being done. These kinds of administrators when working in education or religion are generally without courage; in health care and business they are afraid. No real change takes place because their high-minded neutrality covers up a commitment to the status quo.

Some managers or potential leaders have had too little training or their training was superficial. These managers are aware that transforming an organization takes a lot of skills, and they want to lead but they ask the wrong questions, focusing on how they can lead rather than how they can get others to follow or how to motivate, inspire, and influence them. These *lonely laissez-faire managers* get little done and end up intellectually and spiritually maimed by their own frequent uncorrected failures. Inactivity even by people in top leadership positions is common, and followers get used to reporting to leaders who, although still on the job, have already retired. This is very frustrating, especially when such fearful figures "simply continue in their present understanding of leadership with its behavior patterns, values, and objectives until they retire." Some then continue as members of advisory boards or committees, or as trustees or regents—"polite undertakers of stable and declining or dying" organizations.[18]

The *narcissist* who occupies a leadership role is primarily interested in self-importance and personal fame. At first he or she seems charismatic, his plans grandiose, and her vision compelling. Unfortunately, nothing comes of the hopes that followers place in this pseudoleader because he or she is so focused on self, cannot work with others, and cannot accept input from others; this pseudoleader limits others' energy, contribution, and spirit. The talk is great, but talk is cheap. This "articulate incompetent" does more damage than good to an organization, and it takes years to undo the harm. The narcissist is neurotic, entrenched in resistance to others' ideas, and he or she rarely changes.[19]

Another group of managers or potential leaders see themselves as visionary leaders, rarely asking their followers if they see them in this way. These *deaf prophets* are narcissistic, emphasize their own authority, and see themselves at the top of a hierarchy (hieros=priesthood), like abbots in a secular institution. These administrators can easily abuse others, seeing their own vision, or their interpretation of events, or their direction and course of action as the only preordained path to follow. They think they have special charismatic gifts—a self-concept that distorts their leadership. They presume to know what is in the best interest of an organization and what sacrifices can be imposed on others "for their own good." They can see only the future they want; no one else's view counts at all. Unaware that all authority is not over others but for the service of others, these individuals build myths around their own authority and its importance. However, as soon as an administrator needs to emphasize his or her authority, position, power, and leadership, it is clear there is none. Unfortunately, some followers respond to this kind of leader with total surrender and embrace their own passive status.

Some administrators become passive *observers of an ongoing movement* in their organizations. Although good, intelligent, vital people, they fail to accept leadership either because they are unclear about the needed focuses of leadership, or they are unsettled by the constant criticism directed to many who try to lead, or because in their own hearts they know they do not have the insightful or creative contributions needed to move people to a changed future. Such individuals who lack the confidence to lead often hold on to their positions and thus destroy the effectiveness of those who could lead.

Some managers have significant power, often from the fact that they have the support of their own bosses or trustees. They mimic their own bosses but have no substance. They equate this referent power with leadership, unaware that "the exercise of true leadership is inversely proportional to the exercise of power."[20] These pseudoleaders actually *think they are in control*, but they have no effective influence over followers or the organization's future. With very little justification, some individuals take up an almost sacred role in an organization, and unfortunately followers who are too overwhelmed to challenge them let them get away with it. We must therefore "develop an organizational culture that prevents the leader from believing that his or her position of responsibility is a reason for omnipotence."[21]

The first decade of the new millennium has confirmed the gut feelings of many regarding greed and *lack of ethical commitment* or social responsibility in many contemporary organizations and their leaders. The selfishness reached overwhelming proportions as greedy individuals squandered enormous amounts of corporation money and perks on themselves while treating workers with meanness and disinterest. Cheating, outright lying, and false reporting became the common practices of many. While responses included the idea that we are dealing with a few bad apples, there were certainly more bad apples than originally thought. Government regulation of corporate behavior, legal prosecution of some, and refuge in pleading the fifth amendment for others gave ample evidence that many had no interest in leadership, despised their employees and their needs of just wages and fair pensions, and were pseudoleaders devoid of basic ethical values on which to base their actions. In many organizations, leader pathology is a serious problem. Recent decades evidence examples of leaders overwhelmed by ego, greed, blindness, lack of compassion, and lust for power. Parker Palmer expressed similar concerns, "Whether we think of Congress or the courts, business or industry, the news media or mass entertainment, the church or other voluntary associations, many of us feel deepening despair about the capacity of our dominant institutions to harbor a human agenda, to foster human purposes."[22]

Although we witness many problems in organizations and frequent failures in administrators, we know many men and women who would like to move to a new leadership style. They are motivated by a selfless service of others, feel a sense of call or vocation to leadership, and are striving to live out some of the challenges presented in the chapters ahead.

4. Different Expectations of Leadership

Whatever group we live in, we need leadership. But there has been so much failure of leaders in the past and present that we need to look to the future with radically different expectations. How often do you find that leaders do not deserve that title? How often have individuals you know got away with incompetence for decades? How often have you or your friends provided the successes for which others have taken credit? How often have you or your coworkers been ashamed at what you have let so-called leaders get away with? After over four hundred pages of analysis one researcher concludes, "All too often in this review it seems that the errors of leaders are commonplace, but what distinguishes a successful from a failed leader is whether the subordinates can and will save the organization from the mistakes of its leaders."[23]

For too long we have silently accepted the notion that leadership is a special ability or set of skills or even a position that a few privileged individuals have for the benefit of others. The latter express their appreciation in passivity and obedience. Why do so many leaders, total failures or moderate successes, receive enormous severance packages as if they had transformed an organization? That such leaders have had that much of an impact is simply not true; rather most of the work is always done by others. Yet this is a fundamental failure of a frequent understanding of leadership—that the leader changes the organization as if it were a machine, instead of appreciating that it is alive and that the life-giving changes come from other people in the organization.[24] Leadership is not an individual thing: it belongs to a community and is exercised by that community. Sadly, many leaders actually think they are achieving what is being done by others; they arrogantly take credit for the developments and deny to others their rightful rewards. Reflective followers know otherwise. Moreover, while some leaders can take credit for the achievements of their followers, others blunder their way through decision after decision, destroying the morale and successes of an organization that was successful prior to their coming. "The history of the world is full of such leaders, whose errors of judgment and refusal to listen to the good advice of their followers have left millions of followers as physical, emotional, or economic casualties."[25] Too many leaders are failing to be sources of life. Rather, they bring about death to individuals and their hopes, to organizations and their common endeavors. We need new structures that can call a leader to task. We need leadership, but there is no error-free leader, and we need to approach the whole issue of leadership in a new way that sees it as a way of life that we can live and accomplish together. This will require new styles of life for all involved.

5. What's Missing?

Greenleaf, writing in the 1970s and repeating the idea in the 1980s, referred to the age of the "anti-leader." At times we seem to be experiencing that. We face uncertain times regarding leadership and an unsettling future unless courageous individuals dedicate themselves to a new style of leadership. Anyone who wants to be involved in leadership today must be ready to approach the vocation in a radically different way than has been done in the past. The heart of leadership is not discovered in new skills—although they will be needed, nor in a new paradigm of dealing with others—although that will result, nor in the acquisition of new techniques of collaboration, team building, and consensus discernment—although they will all be required. Rather the heart of leadership is a changed attitude toward others, a conversion, and a new way of looking at the world. Leadership is not achieved by "adding on" to our administrational know-how but by journeying inward and discovering values in one's own heart. The only acceptable leadership today is spiritual leadership.

Titles of several recent books on leadership stress this inner journey and focus on the need for a conversion—a genuine change of heart and mind, a new way of viewing one's role in the world. Moreover, leadership is a way of viewing one's role in the world, not merely one's role in an organization. Some recent books include these emphases: *Leadership: The Inner Side of Greatness; Losing Your Job—Reclaiming Your Spirit; Managing with the Wisdom of Love; Rekindling Commitment; Shared Values in a Troubled World; Leading with Soul: An Uncommon Journey of Spirit; Leadership from the Inside Out; The Inner Work of Leaders; The Spirit of Leadership; Leadership and Spirit.*[26] These extraordinary titles stress the increasingly common conviction that "the heart of leadership lies in the hearts of leaders."[27] So, these books and others like them focus on components of spiritual leadership and speak about moral values, ethics, resources of our hearts and heads, the joy of a leadership mind, the need to face the world with soul, the challenge to bring love, spirituality, and virtue to contemporary organizations. Their authors write to counteract "the crisis of spirit in the workplace," to counter "the erosion of spirit and the pattern of thoughtless dishonesty," to refocus leaders' energy because so many have lost their way, "lost touch with a most precious human gift—our spirit."[28]

Why is it that so many administrators today are overwhelmed by stress, that their work frequently brings out the worst in them, that many executives find the need to deaden their pain with unhealthy excesses of sex, drugs, or alcohol? Some seem so restless, without peace of mind, unreal, as if they have lost their inner selves. So many administrators have fooled themselves, and continue to do so, thinking that power, prestige, and position are the indicators of leadership, and that important promotions, increased salaries, and large numbers of dependent employees are the proof of successful leadership.

Many organizations experience crisis, and the crisis is especially a lack of leaders. Today many key people do not take their leadership responsibilities seriously. Each crisis is opportunity for a new approach to life, an occasion for life-producing change. After all, the word *crisis* comes from Greek and simply means "judgment." It is a time to refocus one's mind and motivation and perceive what truly needs to be done. Leaders are born in crisis, and without crisis there are no leaders, just managers. While many organizations are immersed in tragedy there are many potential leaders who if they accept the call can lead others to faith and hope.

What is it that needs to be said today to so many struggling potential leaders? What sort of leader would you like to see today? What kind of a leader would you be willing to follow? I think a leader should be a person of competence, quality commitment, with a sense of responsibility for the organization and its people—all these qualities for sure. In addition, I would like to see positive thinking, creativity, integrity, persevering dedication to the organization's vision and mission, and the establishing of decision-making processes that facilitate all this. However, all these qualities assure us of no more than a fine manager. I would like to be sure that a leader is credible; I would like to know what motivates a leader; I would like to be persuaded that a leader is a person with a sense of vocation and destiny; I would like to be convinced that a person has journeyed within self and there found core values that nurture all else. Put another way, "Heart, hope, and faith, rooted in soul and spirit, are necessary for today's managers to become tomorrow's leaders, for today's sterile bureaucracies to become tomorrow's communities of meaning, and for our society to rediscover its ethical and spiritual center."[29]

Knowing that quality leadership lies within the heart, soul, and spirit of a leader necessitates making a spiritual pilgrimage, not to some distant, unknown land, but a lonely and very personal journey to the depths of one's own being, values, motivation, and destiny. Such a journey does not offer us additional ingredients to our notion of leadership but presents us with an altogether different recipe for leadership. It does not challenge us with a new strategy for success in leadership but trains us to an awareness that our personal life precedes all strategies and gives them focus. It does not update us for the next stage in our resume and career advancement but refocuses our way of seeing things for the rest of our lives. One emerges from this journey with character, a fresh sense of responsibility, a passion for the service of others, and a restless commitment to one's motivating vision. This journey is dangerous because it will call us to change and maybe abandon what we have cherished for so long. For those who have the courage to embark on this spiritual expedition it will be a breakthrough journey that leads to enlightenment, to the discovery of one's true hopes and calling, to a refocusing of one's attitudes to life. A person who makes this journey will never be the same again.

6. This Book's Approach to Leadership

Studying leadership is an energizing and mysterious undertaking. There are so many exciting ideas but often models are too complicated to be useful and qualities too many to be adequately lived by any ordinary person. But leadership does refer to the commitment of ordinary people in their ways of proceeding, of being people at the service of others, of effectively working with others for the attainment of common goals. This book will focus on the basic, simple, yet powerful challenges of spiritual leadership which is at once an image, a symbol, and a model of contemporary leadership challenge.

A common thread in leadership studies is that *leadership is a dynamic process* of constant growth. Individuals need not focus exclusively on the end vision—even though its attainment can energize, but rather the focus is on one step at a time. The goal is not total transformation but a dedication to daily renewal. Spiritual leadership is a form of ongoing daily conversion.

A further question to arise is what is the *hierarchy of values* individuals establish in order to arrive at a commonly agreed goal of leadership. While every theorist has a list, there are some common themes as we shall later see. Certainly these values will come from the inner core motivation of the leader.

Leadership is no longer a lonely vocation of some great person. Rather contemporary studies include a constant dimension of *mutuality*—between leader and follower, vision and all workers, organization and society—each learning from the other. The spiritual leader not only renews self but the community too.

Leadership is a very serious business and it has little to do with the position one holds in an organization. Leadership requires a daily commitment to professionally train oneself in the *needed skills,* to constantly learn, and to be open to new ideas. Being a manager is one thing and many organizations will never need more than a manager, but being a leader is a different calling altogether and it requires unending training in completely new skills that were not formerly needed.

Moreover, theories as a whole, and unconnected insights, both stress that authority and effective leadership do not increase the more power is centralized but the more *power is shared.* Leaders need to transfer power, responsibility, and accountability to workers at all levels. Studies show that the leader no longer organizes the responsibility of workers, a means of production, but draws out vision, ideas, leadership from every worker. He or she must discover the organization's future in its people. To do this the leader will need to establish conditions, build communities, give priority to morale, show reverence, and treat everyone with grace, faith, and hope.

Most significant leadership studies are moving away from how-to projects and centering on the heart and soul of leadership. Leadership exists only when *power and wisdom come together,* and the leader knows both are attained through dialogue among the entire group of employees who have discovered their own self-leadership.

Leadership today needs a change of heart, *a discovery of one's inner self and values*, a renewal, a conversion. Koestenbaum puts it this way, "Leadership requires changing not only the way you think and the way you act, but also the way you will. Leading is taking charge of your will—the innermost core of your humanity."[30]

2

THE SPIRITUAL LEADER

Leadership is not what one does but rather who one has become through the opportunities of interaction with others in organizational life. It is a response to a vocation heard in the depths of one's heart. The results are not simply skills, techniques, or strategies, but rather a mature inner consciousness that starts with "a deep sense of mystery, awe, and oneness with others,"[1] calls the individual to understand that the commitment to leadership implies that he or she has a new set of responsibilities including justice and the personal growth of followers,[2] and opens the leader's heart to a new cluster of values, among which are compassion, inclusion, community, collaboration, spirituality—all connective values. There is true dignity in leadership such as this. The concept of spiritual leader stresses the moral center of the leader, and vision, mission, goals, objectives, and strategies are always checked against the courageous inner mastery of moral commitment. Plumbing the depths of one's own human condition and discovering the core values of human nature enable the leader to integrate personal, community, and professional sides of life. Leadership development is ultimately self-development; it is the discovery of unity and meaning in one's own life, and this leads to the ability to foster these values in others in social and organizational life. No one can be an other-centered leader while fostering distorted self-interested, self-centered biases.[3]

1. The Calling

It is important for anyone working in a position with potential leadership that he or she needs to pause to reflect and to rediscover the importance of a personal calling to leadership.

How you lead is important.[4] Many potential leaders are doomed to a service at the margins of organizational life, a cosmetic role that fails to capitalize on both the opportunity and essential vocation to leadership that their position entails. We need to look at leadership as a call to conversion, a call to see the opportunity and responsibility of leadership as a major contemporary challenge, for so many organizations today are overmanaged and underled. We looked at the fact that many organizational professionals today are visioning their leadership responsibilities as a spiritual and holistic dimension of their lives. Now and again we see an opportunity so clear and significant that we must confront it with all our energy to capitalize on its challenge, and there has rarely been a moment in history as there is today when a comprehensive rethinking of leadership was needed—for everyone for sure, but for leaders in a particular way.

For leaders whose inner values motivate their leadership, Jesus Christ in the Christian Scriptures is their model (see Matt 20:28; Mark 10:45; John 10:15–18; 13:1–5; Phil 2:7). There, Jesus appears as a person of holiness, compassion, and inclusiveness as he fulfils the role given him by God (see Isa 61:1–3a). Many hold on to this courageous leadership style as a developmental process that they can imitate today. When many suggest that the leadership needed today is followership, they imply that the leader who is inspired by Christian values also appreciates that leadership is a form of followership. All Christians feel called to this kind of leadership and reinforce the idea that change is managed upwards, leadership percolates up from the base and does not filter down from some great person whom others presume was born to lead. Of course, Christian values focus on the service of others, demand that we shed self-interest and give priority to other-centered leadership. Many leadership writings today are influenced by Christian values, others are sprinkled with them, like salt and pepper, once the basic ideas are already established. Others today feel convinced of a new challenge to leadership that not only enthuses them but conquers them. It seems to be an answer to a search they have consciously or subconsciously been making. It may well mean letting go of present emphases and following a deeper call. Authentic leadership is not something we do but something we are; it is a passionate response to the yearnings of our hearts. It means we have to unite the major dimensions of our personal, community, and organizational sides of life into an integrated whole, where deep convictions and inner values permeate everything we do.[5] People are not free to lead unless they have discovered deep within themselves the values that give them an enduring purpose, a clear personal mission, and, yes, a sense of destiny. After all, leadership development is ultimately self-development. Spiritual leaders do not just deal with an organization. Rather, they are moral leaders of a culture and stewards of social ideals.

Jesus is the model of leadership—his prophetic action of washing the disciples' feet epitomizes servant leadership (John 13:1–5); and his self-description as the Good Shepherd who lays down his life for his sheep shows the depth of his commitment to his followers (John 10:15). Several times he claimed that he had come among us to serve and not to be served (Matt 20:28; Mark 10:45), a conviction so clear in the early church that St. Paul can insist that Jesus emptied himself to assume the condition of a servant (Phil 2:7).

We see Jesus' leadership in his sharing with others his experience of God. We see Jesus' leadership in his teaching ministry that consisted not in a collection of laws to be obeyed, but rather in a way of life to be imitated. We see his leadership in his ministry of prophetical denunciation of societal injustice and of inauthentic expressions of religion. We see Jesus' leadership in his constant pursuit of a holistic life, not based on rules and regulations but on compassion. We see his leadership in his daily fights against discrimination, in being a voice for the voiceless, in constantly identifying with the marginalized. We see Jesus' leadership not in empty claims to authority but in his ministry of healing miracles. Jesus, our model, is a person of holiness and compassion, of sharing and inclusiveness, of passionate concern for the oppressed, and of courageous challenge to the injustices of institutions. His behavior violates the social norms of his day, defies the parameters of prudence, and confronts the established visions of the social and religious elite. He calls for change, gives a new vision of people's relationship with God and with each other, and challenges institutions, both civic and religious. Morse points out that the Scriptures offer us six components of Jesus' leadership.[6]

1. Jesus' leadership finds its source in a spiritual relationship with God. A leader's authority does not come from position, status, wealth, but from union with a loving God.
2. Jesus' leadership expresses itself in loving solidarity with all men and women. A true leader does not restrict his or her responsibility to immediate followers, but knows he or she contributes to a social vision that impacts humanity.
3. Jesus' leadership offers a new comprehensive way of looking at life, a new model for society. A leader works for change, subverting existing paradigms and offering a new one as part of a vision of renewal.
4. Jesus' leadership challenges the status of the privileged and includes a politics of empowering others. A leader seeks to give voice to everyone.
5. Jesus' leadership presents new boundaries for social relationships. Today's leader rejects stereotypes, breaks social boundaries, and accepts diversity.
6. Jesus' leadership goes far beyond a religious renewal and includes a comprehensive and holistic reform of political, economic, and social systems. All leadership today impacts society at large and must address critical issues in our contemporary world.

Some individuals who think they are leaders approach their leadership like going through a line in a cafeteria, one day choosing to emphasize one thing and the next day another. How can a person create a vision of spiritual leadership if he or she is not convinced of the importance of a spirit of authenticity and integrity in all that he or she does? Some executives have other people waiting on them hand and foot, and it is impossible for them to become great leaders. Manske expresses the underlying idea so well: "The capacity to lead gradually builds over time. However, one's leadership development can be accelerated by constantly visualizing the ideal leadership attributes and modeling one's own behavior after them."[7] Spiritual leaders are critical transformational leaders who constantly reflect on their own motivating vision and daily analyze their own use of power. Their charisma, individualized consideration, and intellectual stimulation are each modified by a life of service to the common good and common vision.

2. Contemporary Challenge

Our society seems at times to have lost its leaders, adrift in a sea of organizational mediocrity, desperately needing leadership to face the challenges of the present and future. The major creeping crisis in many of our organizations today is a crisis of a lack of leaders. Historically we can see so many, even in our own recent experiences, who have frequently made mistaken, unhealthy, unspiritual, nonservice choices for power and control. Nowadays we seem to have become almost comfortable with our leaders' nonactivity, with their lack of creative response to growing needs, and with their fear of making decisions that could receive public disapproval.

Leaders who approach their responsibility with a sense of service in a changing world need a commitment to reflection and prayer to creatively deal with change, political skills to direct the change, and a well-rooted spirituality to be balanced amidst the change. What is your leadership like? Needless to say, a leader cannot initiate spiritual leadership if the organizational culture still has an us-them, top-down, superior-inferior approach.

The history of leadership studies develops from an initial theory that focused on a leader's innate traits to situational factors, to follower attribution, to a combination of traits and situations, to a leader's behavior. Nowadays, leadership scholars distinguish between transactional leadership and transformational leadership.

Transactional leadership is based on an exchange between leader and follower, the latter wanting something that the former has, whether it be a material or a spiritual good. The transactional leader maintains his or her authority by contingent reward (rewarding performance and accomplishment) and by management-by-exception (correcting deviations and intervening when standards are not met). The transactional leader is the bureaucratic manager who uses pay-offs to manipulate followers to attain organizational goals. This is the leadership of a majority in business, politics, health care, education, and, alas, also in many religious institutions.

Transformational leadership provides followers with vision and a sense of mission, inspires high expectations, offers intellectual stimulation, and gives personal attention and consideration to each follower. Transformational leaders are "change agents; they are courageous; they believe in people; they are concerned to articulate core values which steer their behavior; they never stop learning; they are able to cope with complexity, ambiguity, and uncertainty; and they are visionaries."[8] Transformational leaders inspire, energize, and intellectually stimulate their followers. They broaden and raise the interests of followers, generate awareness and commitment to a common mission, stir followers to look beyond their own self-interest, and enthuse them to produce beyond expectations.[9] Transformational leadership mutually stimulates leaders and followers "to higher levels of motivation and morality."[10] Transformational leadership challenges the leader to a change of heart. Many contemporary theories of leadership stress a conversional experience.

Scholars now view transformational leadership as the most meaningful paradigm of leadership, a special branch of leadership, and a school of leadership. Many writings on transformational leadership refer to it simply as leadership. "This terminological shift implies that transforming leadership was increasingly coming to be seen as 'true' leadership."[11]

I think all who take their leadership seriously would hope and claim to be transformational leaders, raising followers to new levels of vision, commitment, and morality. However, transformational leadership also helps followers achieve authentic needs and engages them in a process of decision making and collaboration. "Without genuine collaboration, leadership ceases to be transforming and moral and becomes conforming or ideological,"[12] as the so-called leader expects others to follow his or her subjective understanding of life, mission, and institutional aims. This conforming leadership is oppressive, provokes inauthentic change, is self-centered, and insidiously leaves the so-called leader thinking he or she is doing God's will. Only when there is genuine collaborative interaction does transformational leadership exist. Is your leadership transactional, transformational, or conforming? Transforming leadership is a move from self-centeredness to other-centeredness; it is the beginning of a leadership based on inner values of heart and spirit.

3. Themes in the New Leadership

Developments in leadership studies increasingly focus on transformational leadership, seeing it as a new paradigm of leadership. Leadership qualities needed in the past give way to a new set of skills and talents.[13] These include focus on mission, vision, and the empowering of others; they stress creating commitment, stimulating extra effort, and generating interest in others, and in general taking a proactive approach to leadership.

New leadership focuses on four significant areas of the leader's life—personal talent and abilities—innate or developed, community-building skills, managerial competence, and organizational renewal. Each of these is approached with the specific interests and commitment of a spiritual leader.

A. *Personal Talent and Abilities*

John Gardner lists fourteen attributes of a leader.[14] Many of the qualities are also highlighted by other writers, and so I have listed Gardner's qualities in the first column of the chart on page 24, frequently mentioned similar qualities in the second column, and less frequently mentioned similar qualities in the third column. At first glance some of these qualities appear innate, but all, in fact, can be learned. The former equation of personal innate gifts with charismatic leadership has also changed to a skills approach to charisma.

Personal talents are a significant focus for whether one wants to lead or not. A strong sense of personal identity, core beliefs, and inner standards, a clearly focused personal enduring purpose, an acceptance of one's personal aspirations and destiny, and finally a willingness to go public with them all are preliminaries to leadership. One writer suggests that prior to embracing leadership a person should assess the personal risk involved, the

Attributes of a Leader

Gardner's Attributes	Other Writers' Attributes	Infrequently Mentioned Attributes
1 Physical vitality and stamina	Well-organized life	Emotional stamina
2 Intelligence, judgment-in-selection		
3 Willingness to accept responsibilities	Eagerness	Initiative
4 Task competence	Pragmatic approach	Knows how to get things done
5 Understanding of followers and needs	Participation	
6 Skill in dealing with people	Sociability, popularity, empathy	Cooperativeness
7 Need to achieve	High dedication to the job	
8 Capacity to motivate	Inspiring, alertness to others' needs and motives	Verbal facility
9 Courage, resolution, steadfastness	Determination, persistence, ability to tolerate stress	Learns from adversity; tenacity
10 Capacity to win and hold trust	Decisiveness	Credibility
11 Capacity to manage, decide, set priorities	Clear objectives, timing, responsibility	Sound analytical and problem-solving skills
12 Confidence	Appearance and body language	Internalized self-control
13 Ascendance, dominance, assertiveness	Modeling	Competitiveness
14 Adaptability, flexibility of approach	Effective management of risk, high level of innovation, alertness to and insight into situations	Can seize chances when presented

personal priorities one has, the personal self-knowledge one has acquired, and the personal skills and abilities with which one is equipped.[15] In its early phases, leadership is a response to oneself, one's own responsibility and calling, and only later opens to something larger. One writer refers to this response to one's inner call as a reclaiming of our soul: "it involves finding and fulfilling our life's purpose. This means realizing our values and aligning them with our talents and gifts. It is our unique contribution."[16] However, it is important to check as to whether one has the generally expected qualities for this calling, and the list provided is an initial checkup.

B. Community-Building Skills

A caring leader must be able to mold a community out of followers and reach out to people beyond the immediate group. A spiritual leader sees the organization as an extension of self and treasures the welfare of others as much as one's own. While a leader's talents are important, the age of the solo leader is over and collaborative and community-building skills now are essential. In fact leadership is a relationship in which the individual leader's tasks have been significantly reshaped from what they used to be. In the past they were directive and executive, now they are proactive, collaborative, and delegational; in the past the leader's experience led the organization through well-known situations, now the leader's task is generally to guide through uncharted waters. Recent leadership scholars have noticed changes in the increased importance given by followers to service, cooperation, and family interests. What deadens leadership today and destroys the inspirational values of leadership is a lack of faith in others, an unwillingness to engage others honestly, and being trapped in selfishness—all blocks to building community. While some pseudoleaders will continue to ignore others, suppress their ideas, and even intimidate them, nevertheless, leadership has seen a shift in emphasis from the leader to followers. The leader needs to shift focus from self to others, and that means giving love and encouragement to followers. This love includes a deep understanding of others, a willingness to share ideas and information, a readiness to share deeply personal ideas and feelings, the giving and receiving of emotional support and affection, the vision of growth with and through others.[17] If ambition is still a part of new leadership, and I think it is, then it is ambition for the success of the community or organization of which one is a part.

In practice, these community-building skills include appreciation for every individual and the skill to manage conflicting values, so that different sides can both win in the adoption of a new shared vision. Frequently a leader belongs to several groups within an organization and can become a bridge between them. The leader must be able to overcome the obstacles to creativity in the community. These obstacles include the tradition that we have always done it this way, fear of failure, comfort in the known, lack of appreciation of others' potential, bias for short-term goals, a lack of questioning, aversion to risk, overprotectiveness of the status quo, and a lack of modeling by the leader. Creativity means finding alternatives to fixed ways of doing things, and finding those alternatives at precisely the times of crises when reliance on the same old frame of reference is common. A leader becomes a voice, a spokesperson, for the community's creativity, and together they set a new direction for change and renewal. "The perceived paradox between these two aspects of separation—knowing that a leader is inherently separate from you, but experiencing a sense of intimacy and connection with the leader—is what creates a sense of charisma in transformational leaders. There is something appealing about these two aspects combined; either one alone is far less attractive."[18] This discovery of one's greater self within the community is made easier for the leader who has the ability to learn from others, humility, and a little self-doubt to balance the considerable self-confidence that is generally a leader's daily nourishment. Leaders take their work seriously but not themselves, and being the object of honest criticism and even of jokes does not disturb them.[19] These points are not unlike the four strategies that Bennis and Nanus discovered to be central in the activities of ninety prominent leaders: they established attention through vision, created meaning through communication, maintained trust with their people, and knew their own strengths and weaknesses.[20] Such people are given leadership by their followers. When an individual is willing to go deep within his or her heart and speak the truth one finds there with great integrity, others respond to the leader's authority.

C. Managerial Competence

Leaders are more than managers, but they need competence in management skills. They complement their organizational skills with long-term planning that includes critical evaluation and problem-detection skills, ability to both create and communicate vision, to maintain their own leadership image, and the capacity to empower others.[21] Managers today need to be teachers by their example, mentoring, and clearly articulating an inspiring shared vision.

Leaders are also capable of being bridges between their own superiors and their followers—both sides maintaining confidence in the dialogic skills of the leader. A leader respects both superiors and followers, letting them live the way they wish, letting them act as they choose, letting them do the job in the way they see fit. After all, much of what others do is not of importance to the organization—it is simply neutral.

The leader with refined management skills searches out challenging opportunities to change, grow, innovate, and improve. So managerial skills are a given, but the leader looks at each job differently.[22] Perhaps more than anything else, the leader's managerial competence climaxes in the effecting of change. Such a leader must be persistent in working for change, recognize the time when followers are ready for change, provide support during the change, create ownership of the change, and establish new goals after the change. Beck and Yeager believe that this window of potential arises when a manager combines ability (technical skills, interpersonal skills, job knowledge, and organizational power) with motivation (interest, confidence, willingness to assume responsibility, and alignment with organizational goals).[23]

D. Organizational Renewal

A leader is especially a person with a clearly established direction in life, aligns people in terms of that direction, and motivates and inspires them to move in that direction.[24] Obviously, the leader must expect some resistance. In fact, a speaker I heard whose name I forget suggested that if a leader does not lose at least 20 percent of followers because of values, he or she probably does not have any. Clearly, the leader will face opposition and must be resilient and constantly faithful to values. In spite of anticipated rejection, the leader is able to draw followers out of their apathy into a dedication to organizational changes and institutional renewal. This includes broadening the organization's relationship to the larger communities with which it relates.[25]

Frequently, organizational renewal starts when a leader is willing to work outside his or her job description, outside the box established by organizational boundaries, and seeks new means and new goals. This can be uncomfortable, but it is often where effectiveness lies. It starts when a person is willing to change his or her own inner values and beliefs, model them for the followers who can then confirm or reject them, and gradually together align the organization's goals with these changed values. Change starts within the leader's heart. As Bennis has said, "To become a leader, then, you must become yourself, become the maker of your own life."[26]

4. Transcendent Values

All leadership involves change, but not all change initiated by leaders is morally good. Several leadership theorists consider both Gandhi and Hitler as transformational leaders because they both implemented change and did so in ways typical of a transformational leader. What is lacking in several leadership theorists is the appreciation of developmental and sequential stages of leadership. Those like Burns, who do, draw upon developmental psychology and see growth in leadership as a movement away from self-centered isolation to a loving concern for others. "The process of self-transcendence, however, is not a one-time achievement, nor one which, once achieved, is permanent."[27] Growth in leadership parallels a movement away from self-centeredness toward greater self-transcendence in the progressive discovery of others and the world we share. Growth in leadership is an asceticism, an ongoing conversion. It means turning away from autocratic, coercive, and manipulative practices of the self-absorbed—those leaders who are "increasingly dependent on a limited, biased, and completely subjective kind of thinking."[28] Such leaders act as if they alone were the source of truth. Further, growth in leadership means turning toward the world in its distinctiveness and toward others in appreciation and desire for greater relationship. Such leaders are collaborative, value the authentically human in self and others, and empower others. For this kind of person, leadership development, spiritual growth, and human maturing all wax and wane together. So leadership development is ultimately self-development; it is a way of spiritual growth.

Part of leadership is the ability to come up with a new creative synthesis that moves a group to real change and mutual purpose. This is not achieved with information and knowledge but with creative insight and wisdom. It includes the conviction that people and relationships precede structures and their values; the higher values of the common good are more important than obsession with self-achievement; perception becomes more inclusive and diversity enriches the search for solutions. This enables the leader to imagine the organization in a new form, convinced that the organization's future is inventible. This kind of transformational leader lives in a world where spiritual and material values are integrated, where personal spiritual growth and organizational renewal and regeneration go together, where spirituality and scientific ability are two sides of the same coin. Such transformational leaders working in transformational organizations are spiritual leaders. While knowledgeable concerning the present and skilled in organizational change, leaders must be able to transcend the present and move from what is to what ought to be. Many problems within an organization result from a leader's own inner conflicts, or from experiences of insecurity, stress, or control. Such leaders can humbly transcend self's limitations, welcome leadership wherever it is found with the organization, appreciating what Max DePree called the "roving leaders" in our midst, and reach out for the wholeness that the community brings. Leadership is a journey of the Spirit in which the individual leader's commitment to the service of others can be a symbol of the Spirit's healing presence and abundant love. Harrison Owen speaks about the five functions of leadership, viewed from the importance of Spirit:[29] 1. To evoke Spirit with wisdom. 2. To grow Spirit with collective storytelling. 3. To sustain Spirit with structure. 4. To comfort Spirit at the end (when things fall apart). 5. To revive Spirit when grief works.

This Spirit-based leadership is a combination of spiritual and scientific skills that allows an organization to transcend the present and discover its own future. The leader who can transcend self lives energized by faith, hope, and love. This is an inner transformation that eventually mirrors organizational transformation. As Marcic wisely points out: "You can become more spiritual by following a spiritual path, but you cannot use spirituality for your own gain. Instead, love, spiritual law, and virtue can help you to see the essential nobility of yourself and others and apply this nobility to the world of business."[30]

5. Ten Core Values of a Spiritual Leader

A person with responsibility who wishes to work effectively with others for the attaining of common goals knows that personal and work life must be in balance. I suggest ten core values of the spiritual leader that help foster and maintain the leader's balanced life between leadership effectiveness and transcendence of self.[31]

1. **A sense of call and inner integrity.** Great leaders are grounded in motivating values. This is the call to personal wholeness; it is a call to bring hope to situations of crisis. Such a leader's authentic life of commitment becomes a symbol of God's healing presence and of God's abundant love. This compassion includes careful listening, empathy, openness to and respect for the Spirit in others and in their gifts. This implies discernment, self-knowledge, and self-transformation. Fidelity to a sense of call leads to inner integrity and trustworthiness. It will also include a willingness in the leader not to fall too far behind in visioning and change readiness.

2. **Faith in a shared vision.** A dedication to spiritual leadership can draw the best out of both leaders and followers in their commitment to a shared vision, especially when leaders remember they are followers and followers remember they are leaders. In times of uncertainty we need to have faith in the shared vision, for there is no possibility that individuals, no matter how charismatic, can call the shots in a complicated system like today's organizations. The vision has to be something we achieve together, with mutual appreciation, solidarity, and patience.

3. **Nourishing the shared vision and inspiring commitment to it.** Only someone who has crossed the threshold to an enthusiastic dedication to the shared vision can nourish that vision in others. Certainly, a leader must know organizational policy and strategic thinking, but he or she must also know what precedes policy and planning, namely values, vision, and mission. This central task of leadership—maintaining the spirit and vision of the organization—has far more to do with organizational effectiveness than almost any other aspect of organizational development. In this light Greenleaf spoke of "The Servant as Nurturer of the Spirit," the title of an unpublished article of 1986.

4. **Relentless pursuit of a common mission.** This implies fostering self-leadership in followers. Being a visionary is not enough for the leader; he or she needs to have the practical skills to motivate others, and the inspiration to move followers to something beyond their immediate comprehension. The leader must balance a sense of urgency with patience, never allowing one without the other.

5. **Profound sense of community and human interdependence.** Leadership emerges from the interplay between leaders and followers. This will imply open communications and the positive belief in others that leads to the creating of a climate of unity and mutual trust in which the welfare of others is as important as one's own. When a

leader thinks in distinctions he or she is trapped by them. Rather what is needed is a system's orientation in which the community is viewed as a whole, all parts are seen as necessary, and there is lots of room for diversity. This leader values both individuality and diversity. John Gardner suggested that "attention to leadership alone is sterile—and inappropriate. The larger topic of which leadership is a subtopic is the accomplishment of group purpose, which is furthered not only by effective leaders but also by innovators, entrepreneurs, and thinkers; by the availability of resources; by questions of moral and social cohesion."[32]

6. **Humility toward one's own views.** Leaders can never make their own views normative for others. Moreover they need to recall that even the service of others can be dedicated manipulation. Rather contemporary leaders need personal ethics that includes constant self-scrutiny, and that keeps the focus on the common task and not on self. This will include the celebration of others' successes and the realization that autonomy must be pushed down to other equally competent individuals who are followers. The humble leader is the one who can share power with others—for he or she does not cling to it, and is open to continual quality improvement—for he or she never believes it is already attained.

7. **Making a difference in others' lives.** This begins with respect for the dignity of all and an awareness of the importance of empowerment. This will include influencing others to be visionaries, brokering information throughout the organization, using negotiating skills when necessary, and overcoming the hurt in others with healing skills. Focusing on others, individually or through team building, is the primary orientation of a contemporary leader. "Maybe the message is finally getting through that a self-serving style is no longer so beneficial to success in organizations as once thought."[33] The

spiritual leader releases the human energy, talent, and gifts of others.

8. **Having courage to say what needs to be said.** This is the prophetical ministry of leadership. It grows out of inner peace and times of withdrawal for personal quiet time and reflection. It requires courage, for some people will love you for exactly the same reason why other people will hate you.

9. **Challenging others to their best.** Challenging others always requires the skills to criticize constructively, to work for compromise, and to set challenging but attainable goals. It needs sensitivity to timing, and genuine benevolence toward others.

10. **Ability to maintain distance from task and people.** Leaders need time alone when they can stop working and stop thinking and simply renew themselves with the love of their family, inspirational reading, reflection, and recuperative leisure. A leader cannot be a person with a cluttered life and cluttered mind. Rather, he or she must be a person of wisdom, since it is wisdom that allows one to see common themes in disparate ideas, that enables one to solve problems amidst contradictions, that frees one to be appreciative of others' gifts for the common good, that can discern the potential for greatness within the ordinary experiences of daily life.[34] The inner freedom attained in times of withdrawal fosters the outward freedom needed in times of involvement.

Conclusion

To be a spiritual leader is a lifelong task; not a burden, it is the personally enriching call each one of us has received. How one lives one's leadership will teach more than the content of any speeches to others. It will give meaning and direction to our lives, a quality of presence to other people. One writer says, "Spiritual leadership is born through the struggle of leaders to balance the complex tradeoffs of people and systems. Spirituality is evident in the creation of human meaning while satisfying our need for production. It is precisely in the midst of these experiences of adversity and leadership that leaders find their spiritual home."[35] Bolman and Deal express this challenge powerfully: "Heart, hope, and faith, rooted in soul and spirit, are necessary for today's managers to become tomorrow's leaders, for today's sterile bureaucracies to become tomorrow's communities of meaning, and for our society to rediscover its ethical and spiritual center."[36]

Those who dedicate themselves to spiritual leadership end up with a big surprise. Their dedication is rewarded by Jesus in an unusual way. Having spoken of his style of leadership throughout the Gospel, he changes focus at the end. He says, "I do not call you servants any longer,…but I have called you friends" (John 15:15). I also am convinced that as we enter the third millennium with hope, the way spiritual leaders lead others will merit this reply.

3

SPIRITUAL LEADERSHIP

1. The Vision and Values of a Spiritual Leader

A common thread found in the proliferation of leadership studies today is that leadership is not leadership in the way people have typically understood it. This implies that some individuals, considered to be leaders a few years ago, would no longer be viewed as leaders in today's changing situations. Books on leadership used to deal with competition, productivity, structures, power, authority, the executive, what works; then they began to deal with empowering others, motivating, facilitating growth, team work; and nowadays they address issues of creating opportunity for others, learning to lead, anticipating the future the group strives for, delegating, freeing others, influencing others, and becoming a superleader. Thus, the shift has been from the individual leader achieving the goals, to the individual leader achieving goals by capitalizing on others' talents, to the present situation where the leader leads others to lead themselves. He or she inspires them with a shared vision, influences them through faith, hope, and love, changes structures when necessary, and models the way. To put it bluntly today's leader has a new set of skills that enable him or her to get out of the way of the followers. Leadership is no longer the result of skills but of inner values, of heart and of spirit. As Hawley suggested, "The key questions for today's managers and leaders are no longer issues of task and structure but are questions of spirit."[1]

John Gardner quotes H. G. Wells, "Leaders should lead as far as they can and then vanish. Their ashes should not choke the fire they have lit."[2] Unfortunately for some leaders when they have finished, there is nothing left but ashes, and no signs of a

35

phoenix in their midst. Kouzes and Posner, commenting on the
fact that leaders are no longer commanders, controllers, bosses,
or big shots, conclude "they are servers and supporters, partners
and providers."[3] Manz and Sims proclaim that leaders must
"influence subordinates to engage in...self-leadership."[4] Two
commentators on leadership in business conclude, "Being a servant may not be what many leaders had in mind when they chose
to take responsibility for the vision and direction of their organization or team, but serving others is the most glorious and
rewarding of all leadership tasks."[5]

Today's rethinking of the theory and practice of leadership
transcends all emphasis on expertise and management skills.
Rather these are presumed, and today's focus is on a vision that
has always been central to the revelation of Christianity. After all,
Jesus said, "I came to bring fire to the earth, and how I wish it
were already kindled!" (Luke 12:49). "I am the good shepherd. I
know my own and my own know me" (John 10:14). He also proclaimed that he "came not to be served but to serve, and to give
his life a ransom for many" (Matt 20:28). Today's emphases on
leadership can draw the best out of individuals. Joe Batten, who
gave the army their phrase "be all you can be," writes, "If you want
to reap the rewards that justice dictates must always fall to the vic-
tor, you must have the privilege of making a fundamental decision: to expand and empower people, not compress, repress,
suppress, or depress them; to build on their strengths, not focus
on their weaknesses."[6]

The vision of being a contemporary leader is something you
care about passionately, for while leadership can be exhausting,
stressful, and rigorous, it is for the dedicated few a "disciplined passion."[7] It is an enthusiasm from within, since people always want
from you that part of you they do not pay for, your creativity, vision,
enthusiasm, and integrity. Spiritual leadership is not a pious
Christian reflection, it is the center of contemporary reflections on
leadership. Two writers on organizational leadership had this to
say: "And what sustains the leader? From what source comes the
leader's courage? The answer is love. Leaders are in love—in love
with people who do the work, with what their organizations produce, and with their customers."[8] This is indeed a different kind of

response to the nature of leadership than we have been accustomed to in former literature and practice.

However, the authors are not alone in their refocusing of leadership to inner values of the spirit. Peter Koestenbaum wrote that "Leadership is a conversion experience. It is a new alertness. It is a 'snap' in the mind to a fresh reality. This is a breakthrough theme. Its models are religion, art, politics, and love."[9] Once you see leadership as an inner spiritual journey, a personal call and vision of life, rather than a position of authority, or the accumulation of power, influence, and wealth, then both the scholar and practitioner must ask different questions, see hiring, training, and evaluation in new ways, reinterpret the meaning of success and effectiveness, and look to organizational development in new ways. Leadership is no longer a matter of skills and accomplishments; rather it focuses on the ultimate meaning of life, it deals with destiny and one's role in the universe. Reflecting on the plethora of books on leadership, most of which have taken a wrong focus, Koestenbaum says we must go beyond questions of technique to ask deeper, more fundamental questions about leadership: those that address philosophy and speak to core human values.[10] Leadership is not simply what we do, but who we are, and what we do because of who we are. Thus, we see that leadership theory has changed focus and much of it now centers on leadership that emerges from a spiritual commitment. Fairholm captures this change well when he speaks of spiritual leadership as exemplified in servant leadership: "The new spiritual leadership paradigm sees transformation of self, others and the organization as important, even critical. This new leadership model is that of the servant leader. Servant leadership is not an oxymoron, it is a juxtaposition of apparent opposites to startle the seeker of wisdom."[11]

Nowadays, the conversion to quality leadership generally results from a period of seclusion and withdrawal from the clutter of day-to-day responsibilities; often a personal crisis leads to reflection and a new wisdom that helps one reinvent his or her leadership. Genuine leadership today is a self-defining choice, a rediscovery of a sense of call to serve others, and a new focus on what is truly important in life. The inspirational leadership that is needed today results from a sense of mystery, an appreciation of one's role in the world, and a selfless dedication to the human community. It means thinking with your heart as well as your mind. Bausch expresses this forcefully when he too sees spiritual leadership expressed in servant leadership: "In the virtual learning organization of the future, and this will be the dominant form of organization, there will be no viable paradigm of leadership other than servant-leadership."[12]

This chapter offers some of the effects of a commitment to spiritual leadership in the attitudes a leader manifests, some consequences of this commitment, some fallacies that this approach shows up, and the environment that spiritual leadership fosters. The chapter concludes with some short-term goals that someone interested in leadership could work on.

2. Components of Spiritual Leadership

One of the key components of spiritual leadership is *dedicated service.* The spiritual leader draws on the inner values of his or her life and later makes the choice to serve others by a commitment to leadership. Spiritual leadership begins with an attitude; it is a form of service rather than service being an effective way to lead. It is easier to be a servant and to learn how to lead than it is to lead and then to learn how to serve. This sense of service will include a readiness to give attention to the needs of other leaders who report to you.

From the very start of one's leadership of others one must be ready to live with an *honest vulnerability.* The leader recognizes that leadership is a gift and is always aware of his or her own weak and lonely experience of self. He or she knows there is strength in discipline but also in honest vulnerability. Leadership is not a way to power over others but a call to nurture the gifts of others. It means letting go of the desire to be always right, or to always have the answers. Successful leaders who admit their mistakes clearly earn more respect from their followers than do those who unsuccessfully try to hide them. Some mistakes cause pain to others, but a good leader can acknowledge wrongdoing and genuinely apologize. However, the leader also experiences the pain of failure without becoming insecure, and he or she can bounce back from suffering with an appreciation of how other people feel in times of hardship. Each one must ask if he or she is comfortable or afraid to let others see his or her leadership weaknesses. Of course, if a leader cannot accept his or her own limitations, he or she will probably have more difficulty accepting the limitations of others.

One quality that followers expect to see in their leaders before all others is *inner integrity*. Credibility is the foundation for leadership. People want to have faith and confidence in their leaders, for they must know in their hearts that their leaders can be trusted. Followers understand that how a person does something says a lot about his or her values. Leaders must continually ask themselves what grade on trust and credibility other colleagues on an administrative team or followers would give them. Inner integrity includes being accountable to others and to a shared vision.[13]

Commitment to example can have a powerfully pervasive influence on an organization, even though it is generally haphazard and unsystematic. Modeling leadership is now viewed as one of the four prime responsibilities of anyone in authority. Manske suggests the following ways in which a leader can set an example worth emulating by followers: Be totally dedicated to the job, choose a high-quality staff, keep cheerful, don't "pass the heat," acknowledge mistakes, avoid criticizing others, work hard and smart, refrain from office politics, stand up for principles you believe in, be open-minded, diplomatic, positive in your attitudes, energetic in your work, a team player, and be enthusiastic, respectful of workers, and never become comfortable in your job.[14]

An important complement to example is *coaching and guiding participation*. This complements modeling, providing task direction, goal setting, reinforcement, and helpful criticism. It means observing everyone astutely to identify their gifts and needs; it means building alliances and developing partnerships. This kind of leader can identify the strengths of others and let go of his or her own position in favor of someone else's. Such a leader can rejoice in other people's growth in leadership rather than be threatened by it. Such a leader need not be overly dependent on verbal communication but has the patience to wait for others to learn from example.

A further key component of quality leadership is the ability to *create a climate of mutual trust.* Without this an organization is filled with suspicion and vision is lost. A leader needs to treat everyone graciously and maintain trust with those above him or her and those below; at one time a leader and at another a follower, he or she enriches the organization with increased trust levels. It is always interesting for a leader to ask whether people enjoy working with and for him or her. A leader must make decisions but the approach to decision making can be a key component of spiritual leadership.[15]

Influencing others to be visionaries is a part of the selfless dedication of a spiritual leader. "To be effective a leader must successfully influence the way people influence themselves."[16] This requires of the leader that he or she be present to others, giving time and effort to facilitating the surfacing of their vision, and also that he or she has the ability to clearly articulate a credible vision for the future, and to enthusiastically motivate others to join in that shared goal. Attaining a vision implies changing both behavior and knowledge, facilitating a genuine freedom of expression and communication in the working environment.

The leader must develop strategies *to foster self-leadership in followers.*[17] No period should pass without asking if one can identify exactly what has been done to encourage self-leadership in others. It will require that a leader have trust in self and be peaceful about his or her own leadership; it will require that a leader spend quality time with followers, facilitating others' leadership. It begins by insisting that followers take responsibility for their own effective performance and avoid common responses of blaming others for failure. A great leader is always ready to step back and welcome the birth of new leadership in former followers. In fact, a spiritual leader has no interest in generating an expansion of power, but in sharing power beyond self.

Every leader will always be confronted with the question of *reliability in moments of truth.* Followers will examine how a leader spends time, what questions he or she asks, how he or she reacts to critical incidents, what he or she rewards, and so on.[18] These are among the critical moments of truth in which a leader manifests or betrays what he or she really thinks. In other words, when one's defenses are down, what are one's real values? This reliability at times will include pain, but the leader bears the pain rather than inflicting it on others.

Inspiring commitment to the shared vision brings together many of the values of a gifted leader. While truthful, competent, and decisive, the leader must also be a source of inspiration to search for a long-term future beyond the restrictions of the present. Of course, the inspiring leader is not necessarily at the top of an organization, but frequently in the middle, inspiring in both directions. A vision that is worth effort can only be attained by people working together. So, a leader has to turn followers loose, give them enough room, and let them build up parts of the vision that the leader never envisioned alone. Inspiring commitment to a shared vision means building hope and confidence in others. When people leave the presence of some leaders do they have a task, or when they leave the presence of others do they have a vision?

Showing love and encouragement is the essential for spiritual leadership, and the spiritual leader's love shows itself in deep understanding of others, in sharing ideas and information, in giving and receiving emotional support, in giving help to others and also letting them know that they are needed. Loving and encouraging approaches are more effective than are adversarial ones, and give the leader far more ability to influence others and draw the best out of them. Love fosters discretionary commitment whereas its absence assures the minimalist dedication necessary to preserve one's job. Koestenbaum says, "Love means service, mentoring, seeing the world from others' points of view, making others successful. It means compassion. Love also means validation."[19] So love is not passive; rather it can call leaders to challenge others assertively. These are strong qualities, for there is no pity in compassion, and no sentimentality in love. This love is particularly important in times of transition and in times when followers are in pain. A spiritual leader can enter the sufferings of others, participate in their transitions, while all the time developing a vision of a loving community. When people leave the presence of a great leader they know they are loved. John of the

Cross, a great mystic and an extraordinary and effective leader, says, "My occupation: Love. It's all I do."[20]

The spiritual leader makes sure that other people's needs are being served, that followers are growing as people under his or her leadership. A good leader takes care of followers and is not taken care of by them. This *caring for followers* must be practical too; leaders must make sure that they give followers what they need, rather than constantly cutting budgets and removing resources. "The new leaders will be those who provide followers with what they need to perform to the best of their potential."[21] Max DePree suggests, "The first responsibility of a leader is to define reality. The last is to say thank you. In between the two, the leader must become a servant and a debtor. That sums up the progress of an artful leader."[22] Every person in a leadership position must ask if he or she has looked after others' needs or his or her own, feathered his or her own nest during time in authority or feathered the nests of others. When a leader cares for followers he or she will motivate them more easily.[23] In fact, deep down most people's reaction is "show me that you care and I will listen to what you know."

Criticizing constructively, while always reinforcing the self-leadership of followers, is a skill that is not easy to develop. The leader who cannot facilitate constructive criticism has problems ahead. Two writers suggest, "Peaceful or bloody, discontent with leadership is extraordinarily high, and leaders had better take note."[24] Two other authors suggest six guidelines for criticizing followers in a constructive way: "1. Provide public praise and private punishment, 2. Punish immediately following the behavior, 3. Focus on the behavior, not the person, 4. Be aware of the absence of information in a reprimand, 5. Strive for balance of positive and negative consequences, 6. Make reprimands contingent upon undesirable behavior."[25] A good leader is sensitive to the timing of criticism and can thus bring up the negative at the right time to see its potential for betterment. Furthermore, "the transformational leader does not engage in negative thinking or other energy reducing activities."[26]

In the first few years of the third millennium we have seen many leadership failures in top administrators whose greed and total disregard of others became one of business' greatest scandals. *Bearing the pain* of an organization's growth and struggles is also a component of spiritual leadership. A leader will need to name the pain, search for response, and facilitate healing. Great leaders do not emerge from a situation that is without conflict or struggle. Rather great leaders surface in times of adversity.

The leader who is motivated by the thrill of faith can excite others with the shared vision by *generating enthusiasm* in all they do together. Enthusiasm comes from the Greek words meaning "in God," for the spiritual leader is motivated by a faith that enthuses others, nurtures their optimism and passion. Leaders today are known for their inspiration, heart, inner spirit, and energy—qualities that help maintain momentum in an organization's pursuit of a vision.

3. Some Significant Consequences of Spiritual Leadership

When the leader shifts focus from self to others *a new ethic emerges*. People do not work less but they do work differently, and included in this difference is the desire for self-expression and self-fulfilment, and the leader must stress the development of these qualities. "Leaders we admire do not place themselves at the center; they place others there. They do not seek attention of people; they give it to others. They do not focus on satisfying their own aims and desires; they look for ways to respond to the needs and interests of their constituents."[27]

A good leader can *create a new spirit* in an organization. Such a leader lifts the spirits of all by enhancing their self-worth and making everyone feel important. He or she makes others feel better about themselves, and makes sure that all treat each other with civility, respectful caring, and even reverence. In fact, a spiritual leader shares power and evidences a spirit of freedom while we have in the last decade seen many who expanded their power and became enslaved to it themselves while their followers ignored it.

A *new notion of authority* naturally arises from the way a dedicated leader works with followers. For such a leader, controlling others never enters the debate; rather the focus is always on reciprocity and mutual respect. Authority is a sacred trust, and it is "for others" not "over others." The leader no longer accepts authority over or power over, but only authority for and power to facilitate the growth of others. Of course, empowerment cannot be taught by people who have practiced disempowerment for years. Thus, the spiritual leader knows when it is good to restrain one's leadership.

The leader challenged by inner values of mind and heart pushes autonomy and responsibility down to others, involving and empowering them in a common vision.[28] Thus, *a new view of shared responsibility* grows up, in which authority is not centralized —that's primitive in today's world; rather it is placed at the lowest level possible. This practice of subsidiarity leads to co-responsibility. This kind of leader is not weak; rather he or she is assertive of the right issues, challenging all to be responsible for shared vision and values. It means calling people to be strong in confronting problems the organization faces.

Since there is no longer true leadership without the underpinning of *a new knowledge and integrated theory,* a spiritual leader facilitates people's willingness to share their knowledge with the organization, aware that everyone's input is part of the mission and vision. A leader creates exceptional moments that bring forth the unanticipated skills and insights of every follower. When this happens, previous barriers become gates to discovery beyond our superficial knowledge of coworkers.

As leadership develops and matures, the leader appreciates that organizations need to become more democratic. Contemporary models of leadership tend to promote empowerment, believing that power is expandable. This *new democratization* is the way to go, thus rejecting any kind of control or elitism whether based on class, wealth, gender, status, or position. Genuine participative teams increase individual commitment to pursue team goals, and it deepens awareness, personal responsibility in decision making, and self-evaluation. Democratization is a dimension of individualized consideration that manifests transformational leadership and lets each individual grow to his or her best.

A spiritual leader appreciates the gifts of all, establishes *a new approach to failure*, in fact, even welcomes it, knowing that if you want to be successful you must learn to fail and learn from failing. This leader appreciates that it is a mistake not to allow others to make mistakes. Thus he or she gives followers some reasonable opportunity for failure without reprimand. People rarely learn from doing things the right way, but they can learn from mistakes, and many mistakes are not destructive of an organization's values and vision. Some dysfunctional organizations love to hide mistakes from boards, from followers, and from each other. The spiritual leader does not divide people into winners and losers, but optimizes everyone's contribution.

A leader guided by spiritual dedication sees an organization in a totally different way than do others. He or she sees *a new grassroots growth*. Instead of a top-down philosophy of control, the leader lives comfortably with a percolating model of leadership. Hierarchies continue to exist but our belief in the efficacy does not. Thus, some models of leadership are countercultural.

The spiritual leader's *new approach to leadership* is one that stimulates self-leadership. Always concerned to discover what needs to be done tomorrow that is not being done today, the leader seeks responses in others. While performance goals will always be important, the leader strives to stimulate self-leadership thinking in all followers.[29] For this to be successful it will include education of the imagination that helps all rearrange elements to construct further possibilities never thought of before, to envision new structures never tried before, and to set in place new criteria for effectiveness never used before.

Leadership today focuses on values that are traditionally considered feminine. This *new focus on feminine values* is giving rise to questions concerning the meaning of power, authority, management style, and so on.[30] After all, power, muscle, number crunching, planning, and even decision making are traditionally viewed as male contributions to authority, but computers can do all this today. The spiritual leader learns some of the feminine characteristics of leadership. Male aggression gives place to supportive interdependence, competition to nurturing, connections, and discussion, domination to power sharing, self-reliance to relationships, position and status to democracy and interpersonal development. The bigger picture emerging is that women's ways of leading will call for a questioning of present beliefs regarding the nature of societal development. Druskat concluded part of her study thus, "in sum, the women in this study preferred interaction that emphasized 'connection over separation, understanding and acceptance over assessment, collaboration over competition, and discussion over debate.'"[31]

4. Fallacies Regarding Leadership

The idea that *leaders empower others* is well intentioned but it is a fallacy. Other people already have tremendous power; leaders simply free them to use the power and skills they already have.[32] So, the leader focuses not on empowerment if that implies giving away power, but liberation. As John Gardner pointed out, "Leaders are almost never as much in charge as they are pictured to be, followers almost never as submissive as one might imagine. That influence and pressure flow both ways is not a recent discovery."[33]

Likewise the frequently stated concept that *the task of the leader is to lead others* is now simply old-fashioned. The leader recognizes that the self-leadership of employees is the organization's greatest untapped natural resource.[34] So, he or she does not lead directly but facilitates self-leadership in others. Let people lead themselves; in most cases they do not need you.

A frequently heard fallacy is that *an organization cannot tolerate dissent.* An organization needs the energizing value of dissent. It is silence, passivity, and apathy that are bad. We need active teams with critical thinking and collaborative skills. The leader does not encourage silent support but discussion and disagreement.

Some individuals who are inexperienced in organizational development think that *management skills will sustain leadership.* This is not so! Management obsolescence is now a given. Managers rapidly become obsolete as their established methods grow old.[35] Many analysts are convinced that management causes most of the problems in an organization. The spiritual leader appreciates that management leads to compliance, whereas leadership leads to shared values in a common vision.

Many immature leaders mistakenly think that *an individual can learn collaboration*. It is not that simple. You must first unlearn noncollaboration before collaboration can begin. This is the pain of conversion. So, for the spiritual leader there can be no collaborative methods on top of an uncollaborative attitude or structure.

In times when people saw leadership as genetic and embodied in the great person theory, they felt that *the leader stands apart from the organization*. Clearly that is no longer the case. The leader must be a part of the organization and not apart from it. Hierarchy is still the dominant model of organizational behavior and structure. Often when people talk about collaboration, they mean a collaborative approach within a hierarchical structure. The word *hierarchy* means sacred and gives the manager the status of high priest.[36] This is a dysfunctional form of leadership today. So, the spiritual leader is not apart from but an integral part of the institution.

An interesting fallacy is that *if you are on top you are the leader.* No! Spiritual leaders surface anywhere in the organization, and it has nothing to do with superior position. Leadership is not a position, or job, or place in the structure; it is a process and commitment, an attitude to life. The spiritual leader knows that no position gives leadership; only a single-minded commitment to grow does.[37]

Leaders must control the organization's development. An astounding fallacy! "Leaders know that the more they control others, the less likely it is that people will excel. Leaders do not control. They enable others to act."[38] Control guarantees the diminishment of excellence. A great leader is one who senses the future mission and direction in the expressions of followers. So, no control, but yes for guided freedom.

In times of reaction to more participative forms of government it is still heard that *power is limited*. Power can be shared, it is expandable. Remember that powerlessness corrupts and absolute powerlessness corrupts absolutely and produces the loss of commitment and common vision. The spiritual leader does not limit power but shares it, giving others control and power over their own lives.

A common fallacy is that *top people in a hierarchy lead their organizations*. The leader does not lead the organization but its people, making a substantial difference to their lives, and they will make a substantial difference to the organization. The leader does not focus on the organization but on its people.

Now and again we hear that *society today needs some charismatic leaders*. No! I think not. Charismatic leaders are generally autocratic, presuming they have the vision while their followers are empty and passive. This is not the approach of a spiritual leader. Rather, charisma is not found in the lone individual but in a developing group.

Coming out of old notions of leadership is yet another fallacy: *once a leader always a leader.* No! Many of yesterday's leaders with all their gifts and commitment intact are simply obstacles in today's institutions. The spiritual leader is always a restless learner.

5. The Environment Created by Spiritual Leaders

In a healthy environment *every individual can act in a free and responsible way*. The leader fosters a freeing and welcoming atmosphere, in which mutual respect for each other's gifts and an honest desire to appreciate the gifts of others manifest the caring for the total reality of each individual. Each one is not only competent and given communication but also has confidence and choice.

In an environment created by a spiritual leader *followers believe their manager is credible*. They are proud of their leader, feel they are a part of the team, know they are appreciated—they have ownership.

One of the delightful characteristics of an environment that has benefited from the guidance of a faith-filled leader is that *all are dedicated to the shared vision*. There are clarity about the vision, consensus on common goals, and intensity of commitment.[39] In this environment the leader can accept constructive criticism in a nondefensive way. Such a leader has the ability to listen, can articulate the vision of the group, and can foster and welcome creativity in followers.

A healthy environment is one in which there is *mutual appreciation*. The leader can enter into genuine conversation with followers since they know that in his or her view no one needs to win. Rather the leader is dedicated to helping others move on. At the turn of the twentieth century bosses could do jobs better than 90 percent of their workers. Today 90 percent of all workers can do their jobs better than their bosses. So let them. Supportiveness is now one of the qualities most desired by followers in their leaders. Spiritual leaders establish a covenant with all their workers.

Spiritual leaders because of their attitude to others *open the door to innovation,* facilitate continuous experimentation, and encourage breaking stereotypes. This means being open to new ideas, surprises, and transitional conflict.

6. Short-Term Goals for Spiritual Leaders

Dedicating oneself to leadership may well be the work of a lifetime, but there are plenty of strategies anyone can implement immediately. These are strategies that get things done but also get an individual thinking in different ways about leadership.

1. **Learn more about leadership.** Study leadership and do not presume you are a leader. Leadership does not just happen. It is the result of studied commitment. You study how to do the job just as a physician learns surgery.

2. **Behave in ways that are consistent with your stated values of your leadership.** Audit your own reactions. Religious traditions have always taught followers to examine their consciences on the failures of the day. Make sure that you examine yourselves on your leadership. That is where you spend most of your day, every day.

3. **Give credit to others whenever possible.** Good leadership is nearly always invisible; someone else gets the credit.

4. **Listen to followers.** Listening creates a different atmosphere and builds strength in others. This means making a deliberate decision to talk less in meetings and listen more, identifying at the end of each meeting what you

have learned from followers. Learn what bugs your people and react to problems by listening first. Genuine listening includes openness to the needs, motives, and hopes of followers.

5. **Establish ownership for everything you do.** This means excelling in communication and collaborative discussion. If institutional priorities are the priorities of only a few, they can neither expect nor do they deserve significant support.

6. **Learn to be an executive.** Be executive not only to your boards but particularly to the ideas and visions of those you serve. Authentic leadership percolates up from the grassroots, it does not filter down from high up in the structure.

7. **Stop making decisions.** Invite everyone to assume responsibility. So, strengthen people by sharing information and power and increasing their discretion and visibility.[40]

8. **Get out of the way.** Examine your organization to get rid of unnecessary rules and regulations that put controls on others' initiative. Belasco suggests, "Restrain yourself from helping people out of their responsibilities."[41]

9. **Insist on serving, even in the face of power.** If your boss continues to be autocratic, you must still live as a faith-filled leader. You may have to tolerate autocratic behavior no matter how benevolent it may be, but you neither have to endorse it nor imitate it. If you work with autocrats do not participate; it will only encourage them.

10. **Improve participation in decision making.** Establish pilot programs within the system or organization. You cannot be a spiritual leader whose leadership includes a vision of service while preserving an autocratic environment.

11. **Make hope a priority.** Affirm people, give them high but attainable goals, challenge and reward especially with natural personal rewards of appreciation. The most significant rewards in working life today do not cost anything. A good leader can maintain a strong sense of urgency to attain the group's goal. This inspires hope in others.

12. **Celebrate your people's successes.** Be a cheerleader, scheduling celebrations at all levels of your organization, and encourage others to do so.[42] Honor people's key achievements with public recognition. Not only celebrate when someone reaches a goal, but also when someone reaches his or her potential. Celebration should not become routine and at times even meaningless, rather find opportunities to surprise people with a celebration of their successes.

13. **Deepen reflection in life.** A spiritual leader is nourished by reflection and knows that vision, creativity, and imaginative resolve come from prayerful reflection. The leap of imagination, the ability to find alternatives that no one else sees, the skill to identify common ground in disparate data—these skills are related to reflection and prayer.

Conclusion

All leadership development is ultimately self-development and little else will help our growth as human beings and as Christians as much as a commitment to leadership. Spiritual leadership is not just another management style. It is the result of a conversion and it begins with a renewal of attitudes. While spiritual leadership is an attractive vision it is clear that not many individuals are willing to become this kind of leader. It is the result of a deliberate personal choice, it requires a commitment in love, and it includes significant sacrifice.

Spiritual leadership is very costly. It is neither a technique, nor a strategy in a long-range plan. It is a way of life, results from conversion, changes the whole focus of one's way of dealing with others. It is also the most significant vision of leadership for the generation ahead. Stephen R. Covey, a great proponent of spiritual leadership focused on principle-centered responses, makes a powerful conclusion in one of his articles, addressing servant leadership, "The Servant-leadership concept is a principle, a natural law, and getting our social value systems and personal habits aligned with this ennobling principle is one of the greatest challenges of our lives."[43]

4

INFLUENCING OTHERS TO BE VISIONARIES

The task of the spiritual leader is to minister in the best and worst of times. This leader is a person of integrity whom followers see as a person of credibility. They expect such a leader to consistently maintain a climate of mutual trust and call the organization to an ongoing conversion to its vision. But vision is not something possessed by a minority in the organization, nor is it the exclusive responsibility of central administration; it belongs to everyone within an organization. If the vision is to be relevant to changing times, it will mean skillfully and responsibly interpreting the vision. In this chapter, we focus on sharing and nourishing the vision with others so that they too become visionaries. Kouzes and Posner insisted that leadership is "the art of mobilizing others to want to struggle for shared aspirations."[1] This can also be a time of mentoring for those individuals who have the skill.[2]

At times, organizations have managers who live in arrogant isolation, failing to see the need for change in themselves and in their organizations. Such managers lack long-term commitment and become obstacles to organizational change and transformation, and their days as leaders are numbered, since it is the essential task of leadership to produce change, whether it be personal, community, or organizational.[3] But to see things that others do not see, and then facilitate the required change, is an eventual component of leadership, for leadership is the restless pursuit of what lies ahead. Reacting to changes that afflict an organization is not enough; a leader restlessly pursues what lies ahead, introducing change wherever needed, and he or she carefully selects the direction that change needs to take. Effective leaders do more than react to what hits them; rather they proactively introduce changes, some of which become the breakthroughs that lead to great organizations.[4] Handy and Bennis put it simply when they say, "New ways of thinking about familiar things can release new energies and make all manner of things possible."[5]

1. Move People Upward and Outward

The first stage in influencing others to be visionaries is to raise people up to an awareness of their dignity and at the same time to move them out from themselves and their local community with an awareness of their responsibility to serve the world's needs. At times, an organization may need charismatic leaders who can manage and motivate charismatic followers. Leadership is not the private reserve of a few individuals, but it is a process dedicated individuals use to bring out the best in their followers. First of all this means letting go of former perceptions and understandings, especially the idea that boundaries are barriers. It means the ability to appreciate the gifts of others and to draw those gifts into the organization's common purpose. "Successful team leaders loosen the reins; they don't drop them."[6]

Moving people up and out necessitates the ability to foster creativity in others. This means giving time to understanding how an employee thinks and behaves. Several great spiritual writers point out that hope is greater than memory. The ability to look creatively toward an as-yet-unknown future is worth much more than summarizing the best of the past. A leader's effective contributions to an organization increase with the leader's ability to accelerate changes. Some people build on experience of the past, bringing yesterday's thinking to today's needs; others start anew without the influence of the past, bringing new thinking to contemporary needs. Change-ready leaders can rethink the way things have been done, can reinvent former answers to contemporary needs. They make decisions for urgent needs in light of a vision of tomorrow, appreciating that there cannot be risk-taking without some errors. Furthermore, change-ready leaders offer guidance to those who stand on the boundaries between past and present, and present and future. At times leaders themselves move across the boundaries, since creative and alternative ways of thinking and acting are frequently found outside the box.

This is a critical time for guidance—it is a time when some are uncomfortable, fearful, unconvinced of the need for change, concerned over the costs of change. Others face crisis with challenge, are excited about new possibilities, invest themselves in the change with its innovative learning, skills, and processes.[7] The former are problem-avoiders who must be converted to relish the opportunities that solving problems, criticizing creative processes, and welcoming change offer. The latter look to the future with passion, boldness, and a spirit of improvisation. Clearly, their courage and competence need to be linked to humility, since not all their efforts will prove successful.

2. Encourage Followers to Welcome Change and Crisis

One of the important ways of influencing followers to be visionaries is the way a leader encourages them to deal with change and crisis, and to handle those special moments when vision can become reality. Managing change well is what leadership is all about. Marcic synthesizes this well when she shows that this part of a leader's commitment includes changes in the physical aspects of the organization—working conditions, financial stability, and so on. It also focuses especially on the intellectual parts of change that lead the organization to new perspectives on their work, innovation, creativity, and an appropriate environment that is conducive to creativity. She further insists that leaders must manage the emotional aspects of change that assure the mutual support, respect, and appreciation that all need. Leaders will also need to overcome resistance to change and foster a willingness to pay the price of change. Finally, Marcic stresses the spiritual aspects of change that produce inner transformation leading to love, integrity, justice, and mutual dignity.[8] Making these changes with followers and managing them well is a way that the leader can establish ownership for the changes.[9]

Major changes that significantly affect an organization are generally referred to as crises. Crisis is defined as "a crucial or decisive turning point," "an unstable condition," "a sudden change in course," "the point at which hostile forces are in a state of opposition." The original meaning of crisis is "judgment," or "discernment." Crisis is a turning point when a new kind of judgment is needed. That is why leadership theorists suggest that leadership emerges in times of crisis; without crisis we generally have simply management. In other words, leadership is the combination of that vision and those skills that empower a person to handle crisis creatively, caringly, and productively. But crises, like most changes, are different now than they used to be. In fact, many former crises are now handled proactively as part of good management, and some former crisis management skills are now left in disuse.

Contemporary leaders know that their effectiveness is linked to confronting crises with style. We still deal with explosive crises that need a leader's immediate and full attention, but we need to redefine crisis based on the problems that a leader meets on a day-to-day basis. The contemporary challenge for leaders is whether they can handle productively the creeping crises that their institutions face in struggling for vision, financial security, market share, and personnel stability. Crisis is now structural and systemic; it is not out there, but is part of who we all are together in an organization. Moreover, leaders do not view crisis negatively but as an occasion when a leader can work with followers to discern a new direction and bring all members of the community to greater maturity in the way they implement a shared vision in times of change.

Again we can see that part of the creeping crisis that organizations face is that leadership is different than it used to be and requires changes in roles and emphases. In fact, leadership itself is part of the ongoing creeping crises in organizations. Leadership used to be presumed to accompany authority and was given to experience, tradition, and institutional positions. No one can live off a title anymore. In fact, authority is now short-term for many; and without them realizing it many people's leadership evaporates and all they are left with is their position. Crisis still calls forth great leaders but now they courageously respond, aware of their interrelatedness with their followers. Leaders today establish directions for their organizations, and they reaffirm confidence in the gifts, maturity, and growth potential of their followers. Such persons see crisis and the disagreement, tension, and conflict that accompany it as part of life. Leaders encourage the participation of all in solving a crisis, avoid the power plays of the needy immature, and dedicate themselves to eliminate any pathological aspects that organizations can evidence in times of change and crisis. In times of change and crisis management, leaders show confidence in followers, channel their gifts, unite them in a common vision, and motivate their commitment.

Explosive crises of the past called forth the lonely visionary whose skill and judgment brought speedy resolution to an immediate and critical problem. Nowadays lonely visionaries cannot answer creeping crises but only communities can do so in their collaborative responses. Spiritual leaders appreciate that their effectiveness depends on their ability to foster a sense of shared responsibility, and to utilize collaborative skills.[10] Good leaders do not anxiously anticipate change and crisis, but rather they enthusiastically welcome them, for these situations give leaders significant opportunities to model, and to coach others through times of change while preserving the essential characteristics of a shared vision.

3. Identify a Shared Vision

What is vision?[11] A vision articulates what an individual or organization wishes to become. Having vision essentially implies seeing what others do not see; it means appreciating the beauty, hope, and challenge that new ideas can bring to individuals and organizations. It is a form of wisdom to really know where one is going—even amidst ambiguity, conflict, and constant change—this gives one authority with others. Vision includes the ability to see the big picture, all sides of an issue, to let go of vested interests and eliminate biases, and thus to avoid problems that arise from short-sightedness and parochialism.[12] Frequently, it refers to the future and implies that a leader acts proactively; it then brings out the best in oneself and in others. Increasingly, it means having insight into present realities and capitalizing on some immediate perspective that others do not appreciate. Vision is not simply the prolonging of the present but the rethinking of the whole immediate reality. Vision becomes an attractive and attainable dream. While unsettling and seemingly dangerous, it is constructive of the future. Vision can also be retrospective, analyzing untapped energy in past failures or shortsightedness in leaders who could not see. So vision can be exercised toward the past, present, and future; it is retrospective, perspective, and prospective.

More importantly nowadays, vision is not only seeing in a way others do not see, it is a deliberate decision to look at things in a new way. It starts with one's basic values and one's deliberately identified purpose in life. These two facets of one's personality together form one's philosophy of life. These lead to one's sense of mission or destiny, and out of this come goals and strategies. Vision as a deliberate effort to look at things in a new way is personal wisdom and guides one's own life. Burt Nanus suggested that a leader will know a new vision is needed when, 1. There is evidence of confusion about purpose, 2. Employees complain about insufficient challenge, or that work is not fun anymore, 3. The organization loses its competitive edge, 4. The organization is out of tune with trends, 5. Employees lack pride in the organization, 6. People avoid risk, 7. There is a lack of shared progress, 8. There is a hyperactive rumor mill.[13] If it is self-centered, then the vision can be bad; if it transcends self in concern for others, then it can be good. For leadership to exist, other people must buy into the leader's vision. Then it not only affects the leader, but motivates and energizes others. Such a vision is specific enough that it guides the leader, but vague enough that it suggests courses of action, and brings forth the best from others in its ongoing development. Manasse saw visionary leadership as four interlocking components—personal vision, organizational vision, future vision, and strategic vision.[14]

Vision is not what you see but how you look at things; it's not what you think but how you think; it is not that you see the future, but how to respond to the future; it is not that you appreciate community, but how you see others interacting as a community; it is not that you see things clearly, but that you look at things in the context of the big picture. "Vision is not necessarily having a plan, but having a mind that always plans."[15] This kind of visioning energizes workers and gives meaning to their work of sharing in a vision that becomes a communal standard of excellence.

When a vision eventually comes together, it must be powerful enough to take hold of an organization and its common purpose and goals, to capture people's individual and common hopes, to challenge and stretch everyone in the organization, to energize professional and discretionary commitment, and to satisfy the hopes and longings of all who share it. A vision is always specific enough that people can grasp it and appreciate its sense of direction, yet vague enough that everyone can find a contribution in it that they can make. However, as already stated, a vision for an organization is useful only if followers buy into it. Moreover, once a vision is defined, it must be redefined continually through the new insights of all members of the organization. Although others continually refocus the vision it is still the community's vision, and a leader must always be able to articulate it. In other words, a vision is never final but is open to further clarification. Common values find new ways to express themselves. Values are the way individuals and organizations measure the rightness of their direction. Values do not create vision, but they always measure the authenticity of new articulations.

4. Train Others to Be Visionaries

Clearly an individual can have a vision for his or her own life with little impact on others. In other words, vision and leadership do not have to go together. Healthy hermits have vision. When we speak about vision and leadership, we imply that the leader's vision is shared with others who are also inspired and motivated by it. For any leader who believes his or her vision has value for others, he or she must give others the time and space to identify the common vision and make it their own. A leader can initiate this process, encourage people to question and challenge the status quo, even gently motivate and persuade others as to its values, but can never impose the vision nor allow it to override the visions of others. In fact, a leader will have to let go of his or her individual vision so that it can gradually become the group's vision. Ownership of a vision must be enthusiastically discovered by each individual, changing mind and mind-set, buying into a new way of looking at reality.

Sometimes members of an organization believe in the common vision, but they do not understand it or live it, nor do they understand its implications, nor would they know whether the vision was actualized or not. In fact, they simply presume it exists. This is not enough because not all visions become reality. A leader must facilitate commitment to a shared vision.[16] These visionary leaders are not born but self-made. They bring people together into a cohesive group through dedication to common, basic values, and shared purpose in life. It is these common spiritual values that generate commitment and energize people, create meaning in their lives, establish standards of excellence, and bridge the present and the future.[17] When this is done successfully, visionary leadership is made visible, and the transformative impact on individuals and organizations is exceptional.[18]

A leader needs communication skills to both convey and maintain a vision, needs impressive management skills to maintain the charismatic image, and needs empowering skills to assure participation.[19] Leaders must also live in a state of continued dissatisfaction with things as they are, knowing that to be fully satisfied means to have lost vision. Since training others to be visionaries means helping them to be proactive, the leader must help others to anticipate problems and responses. A leader must surface new ideas in others and celebrate them when discovered. This outlook is particularly evident in times of crisis and chaos, when one order is passing and another has the chance to come forth. Leaders' guidance and vision are critical at such times, when groups move to alternative consciousness and perception from that of the surrounding culture.

Leaders serve as facilitators and animators of a common vision. They know that no individual owns the vision to share with followers, but that the vision is built around that shared identity of the group. Shared values in a healthy corporate culture are the most important unifying force of the group. A good leader will achieve this through a process of vision development.[20] The group participates in predetermining the vision by either their involvement or apathy. Sometimes a group will need a leader to identify their distinctive contributions, selecting, synthesizing, articulating, and revising the group's values. Groups often cannot express their own mission, but they can recognize it when a leader they trust articulates their enduring values for them. As Koestenbaum points out, "Leaders grow by accelerating experience."[21] Thus a leader can focus others' attention and create in them a pervading passionate commitment for a vision that is unknowingly within them. A leader attains consensus by making conscious what lies unconscious in the followers, calling them to articulate what is important to them in the core of their being.

Identifying a shared vision will require collaborative styles of learning, new group techniques for sharing ideas, and new skills of consultation, dialogue, group goal-setting, and strategic planning. The group together seeks solutions, finds the common ground of unity and community, and searches for the synergy that common problem solving and planning can produce. These creative forms of collaboration expand the group's thinking, and can generate new meaning to the group's decisions. These early efforts to identify a shared vision, what one author calls "creating appreciative learning cultures,"[22] is an experience of interdependency.

The leader will push down as far as possible not only consultation and decision making but also planning, strategizing, and goal setting. The team or group takes over the role of the hierarchy in an organization. However, to assure that the vision is shared within the organization, the leader will train groups to keep others in the next group above or below them informed about the essential components of the vision. Indeed, Berson and colleagues conclude that a vision is stronger when it has a series of qualities: "Indeed, inspiring visions should be optimistic, express confidence, highlight the intrinsic needs that can be met, connect to the core values of the organization, and place emphasis on positive future challenges and opportunities."[23]

To identify a shared vision, a leader appreciates that the vision must turn inward to the group, but the focus must be on the people who are served by the vision. He or she will take the vision seriously enough to seek out needed resources to attain it. Identifying a shared vision cannot be restricted to one's working life since a vision that enthuses people will do so because it touches their core values that will be the same in personal, community, and social life.

Groups do not pursue a vision that they do not own. Vision refers to what a group is convinced it should be doing in a given time and situation. Leaders must generate ownership of the vision they find in themselves and their followers; and this can take a long time, and much patience and fortitude.[24] It is often said that leaders must leave followers a legacy, and surely it is the legacy that everyone has a part of the vision; everyone is individually important to the common enterprise.

5. Coach Your Followers Carefully

As people move up and out, leaders need to coach them. Change-leaders encourage their followers to look at things in a different way. This means understanding followers, the way they think, and the way they do things. It implies training them to go away from present views at least long enough to be influenced by something different. But coaching must be done skillfully, and it generally implies giving people important work to do, discretion and autonomy over this work, visibility and recognition for what they do, and the know-how to establish connections with people of power and position.[25] Coaching followers requires strategic skills—modeling a form of leadership based on vision and values, establishing trust among a group of followers, training in team performance, collaborative learning and partnership building.[26] A leader needs to allow followers to improvise and then to learn from their success and failures. There is no risk-taking without error, but no newly created future without risk-taking. Above all, a leader who wishes to coach others to be visionaries must let others have control over their own lives, for it is this sense of freedom that capitalizes on an individual's energy, creativity, and enthusiasm. When a leader can encourage a sense of risk and improvisation in others and link these approaches to humility, then provided there is a solid foundation of competence and genuine perseverance in dedication to values,[27] a leader can unleash profound power, passion, boldness, and courage in the organization. McLean and Weitzel suggest six steps to unleash leadership potential in oneself or others: 1. Practice influencing others, 2. See similarities between self and others, 3. Recognize and meet others' expectations, 4. Accept and let go of leadership roles, 5. Provide support for each other, 6. Always know your own worth and accept your own stature.[28]

Coaching others requires that leaders be reflective, have political savvy, and maintain spiritual depth. Reflection is needed to receive creativity, political savvy is needed to deal with and direct the resulting changes, and spiritual depth is needed to preserve balance and perspective amidst the change. Coaching others presumes intensity of conviction in the leader who is striving to manage, then empower, and finally liberate the performance of others. Intensity of conviction is very subjective, self-confident, and can be influential, and it must be managed by a genuine respect for others and their views, an attitude of benevolence toward others and their as-yet-unknown responses, and an openness to be changed by others' input.[29]

Coaching others means helping followers see the excitement that comes with change and crisis and training them to invest in innovative skills that give the ability to provide alternative solutions that others do not. Coaching others means challenging others to exceed their potential and in doing so exceeding one's own. All this is part of serving others in new circumstances, even relishing change because it gives opportunities to serve perennially in different situations. Approaching change in this way requires humility, passion, boldness, and courage. Coaching for times of change means helping followers retain high levels of self-esteem, intensity of conviction, and self-confidence linked to humility. It also insists that simple aspects of life should not be neglected—appearance, verbal skills, body language, patience, politeness, and civility.[30]

Managers quickly become obsolete, whereas leaders know their tasks are ongoing. They continue to form, support, and coach the new leaders to whom they delegate responsibility. The goals of leadership outlive the leader in his or her followers. However the leader does not withdraw after delegation but continues to be supportive by fostering personal growth and deeper understanding, offering feedback, and building new skills in followers.[31] Leadership means giving your best and getting others to give their best too.

Dedicated leaders live in a state of continued dissatisfaction with things as they are and are always striving for something more from themselves and their followers.[32] To be satisfied would mean losing the vision. Thus, leaders continue to model the vision, to proclaim the ideals of the organization by building up its image, to transmit a shared vision with persuasiveness and inspiration, to demand high expectations of followers, to support followers with high levels of confidence, and to motivate others to the best of which they are capable. A leader helps followers grow in their own leadership style, stressing the ongoing quality of their work, their organizational and societal contributions, and their quality life. A leader will always need to show flexibility, seeking each follower's way of leading. The only part of vision in which the leader shows no flexibility is the continuing need for commitment to values.[33]

Conclusion

The leader's task is to influence others to be visionaries. This requires prodigious energy and a spirit of selflessness. Such a leader can manage an organization's meaning and purpose, can constantly focus people's attention on common values, can manage trust throughout the structure, and can manage the strengths and weaknesses of himself or herself. The lone charismatic leader may well gain visibility, power, prestige, and self-satisfaction. However, the leader who is faithful to a calling will make community central and not himself or herself, will share the leadership of his or her followers and not his or her own position, will work for his or her followers' achievement and not his own, will dedicate his or her life to the growth of others. For such leaders, their leadership will be a heated affair, full of exhilaration and fun. But it will also be exhausting, stressful, and rigorous. For such leaders, "leadership is a disciplined passion."[34]

5

LEADERSHIP AND INTEGRITY

1. The Need of Integrity

Recent years evidence a series of shifts in the values people expect to discover in their leaders. Among the shifts we see new emphases on others, on service, on collaboration, and on family values.[1] Some values seem to be perennial, among which we find respect, honesty, and integrity. This shift in values is part of recent theories of leadership that emphasize followers' attributions to leaders, seeing leader-follower relationships as critical to the understanding of leadership.[2] Nowadays, people want to see that their leaders are genuine, do not need to defend every issue that is questioned, and can maintain their values with humility. Some followers trust a leader based on experience; nowadays followers trust as an act of faith in the sincerity of a leader's proclaimed values. "To become a leader, then you must become yourself, become the maker of your own life."[3] So, from this perspective, two attitudes are critical to leadership, personal integrity in relation to one's vision of life, and integrity in relation to the organization's primary values, issues, and loyalties. People need to know that their leaders are credible and are true to themselves in what they convey by word and life. Integrity is a constitutive component of leadership. People want to have confidence in their leaders, knowing they will consistently live according to the vision and values they proclaim. Since being an agent of change is essential to leadership, people need to be assured that the individual leading them through change is a person of integrity in terms of the communal vision and values. "Credibility is based on trustworthiness (honesty), expertise (competence), and dynamism (inspiring)."[4]

While not necessarily using the same vocabulary used in this book, followers everywhere are seeking spiritual leadership. So, "Mature leadership is an expression of a well developed and defined sense of vocational integrity."[5] Wise transformational leaders who need to constantly deal with ambiguity, with change, and frequently with conflicting solutions need to be people of integrity. Then when they see solutions others do not see, their followers will still trust them. The indispensable quality for leadership that holds everything else together is integrity, the balance between personal and public life. Way back in the seventies when Stogdill reviewed trends in leadership he concluded, "Intellectual fortitude and integrity of character represent traits which are apparently associated with eminent leadership in maturity."[6]

Although integrity is so central, we also must acknowledge that people are not finding it, and they are crying out for it. We all know individuals who had potential as leaders but never achieved a position of recognized faithfulness and integrity. We talk about striving for excellence, but we know there is a lot of rottenness. Some seem intellectually or spiritually maimed by inappropriate training. Some potential leaders continue to do what they have always done and find enough work to keep themselves busy, as the thoughtful, polite undertakers of stable, declining, or dying organizations. Some leaders practice selective perception, only seeing what they want to see, seemingly unaware that 85 percent of all problems in an organization are caused by management. Afraid of the future and insecure in interpreting the vision for changing times, some cling to nonessentials. Some leaders still manifest the kind of neutrality that hides a commitment to the status quo, and followers quickly perceive the lack of integrity. However, we need also to acknowledge that followers sometimes have such deep needs that they grant credibility to a leader even though they know integrity is lacking.

We have some great leaders in every walk of life, but besides them, we often have a lot of mediocre personalities in situations where they claim to be leading others who are clearly ahead of the leader. The increasing problem of burnout in leadership, spiritual impoverishment in some cases, a passive stance by others, lower levels of self-esteem, have all weakened integrity.

Some leaders feel their lives are controlled by outside forces. Others, while achieving institutional goals, do not seem to attain their own full potential. Some knowingly live with "organizational disabilities,"[7] without the courage to confront or challenge. Some current leaders, facing insecurity and challenge, generate myths about their own authority and expect followers to believe them. Others have had serious problems, suffering as they do from the tyranny of petty laws. They allow structures and systems to continue when it is clear they are not working, and yet they are unwilling to change the organization and its culture. Others are dominated by causes and not by the pursuit of truth. Some traditions have a distorted understanding of their leaders, turning them into gurus and myths. Some organizations intended to facilitate the charismatic end up obscuring it, promising care but delivering control, insisting on service but emphasizing authority. In all these cases integrity is sacrificed.

Leaders in dysfunctional organizations frequently strive without success to generate the integrity that leads to trust. Trust is born from a combination of integrity and competence. Without integrity there is no trust. Polonius in *Hamlet* expresses the ideas succinctly: "To thine own self be true, and it must follow as the night the day, Thou canst not then be false to any man." When workers practice secrecy, live in constant competition and jealousy, and do not show mutual respect, appreciation, and support, the resulting attitude is negative, evidences fear of rejection, and creates a sense of constant mutual distrust. Some managers become bureaucrats who give inadequate attention to followers, are unavailable for interpersonal reactions because of constant meetings, and ask for mere token involvement by others—attitudes that followers readily recognize and repay with distrust. Some managers do not trust others enough, claim authority in nonessentials, and lose themselves in organizational trivia. They end with inadequate time for their own personal growth and for quality time with others—attitudes that generate the same responses in followers. The lack of trust leads to fragmentation, competition, and reactiveness.[8] When a leader pays lip service alone to the idea of creating an environment of trust, the followers give only lip service in return.

Leaders who strive to be recognized for integrity must build trusting environments around them. Leadership is achieved together, and it implies a bonding with others. An organization with a trusting environment appreciates diversity, shares values and vision, fosters good clear communication, and mutually challenges members to their tasks. It is at the same time centralized and decentralized; the leader appreciates that excellence in building a trusting environment demands constant focus on organizational culture. Today's leaders must see themselves as creators of the values, mission, and spiritual dimension of an organization's distinctiveness. In fact, they must have the courage to create a loving environment, constantly aware that "A loveless organization has selfishness, political infighting, petty jealousies, lies and distrust."[9]

When a leader wishes to foster trust, he or she must highlight the positive, give clear visible evidence of trust, respect others' freedom, handle their mistakes well, and be ready to compromise to meet consensus. Trust includes the acceptance of risk—letting others be free enough to make their own choices and decisions. A leader must eliminate fear in the organization, create an atmosphere of interdependence, make it obvious that he or she appreciates the gifts of others, and that he or she yearns to collaborate by sharing concerns, values, and vision. The leader will need flexibility in dealing with others' approaches, and a facility in living with ambiguity and tension as a step on the road to shared commitment.

Trust comes—and an acknowledgment of integrity will follow—when followers become convinced that a leader is worthy of them, that he or she approaches issues with well-established prejudices of people over laws and collaboration over autocracy.[10] Nowadays, followers trust an effective transformational leader who maintains a healthy concept of self, community, common vision, and mutual responsibility.[11]

Trust implies a confident hope in others, relying on their authenticity and integrity—at times even before they have proved it. It is at the same time an expectation and an obligation—the emotional glue that binds leaders and followers together. Trust is earned by taking risks—allowing others to make their own choices. It implies treating others as dependable, deserving of confidence, and reliable. Trust is the foundation of collaboration and partnership in a shared vision and a common mission.

2. The Nature of Integrity

Integrity requires courage to speak the truth, to accept one's own independence and autonomy, to honestly present the implications of a vision, and to faithfully persevere in the demands of a vision even when it means standing alone. Integrity includes accepting one's own blind spots, in abilities and failures. Integrity is primarily an inner self-knowledge but also refers to followers' perception that leaders' values and actions match their words. It is a form of holistic living. One writer says: "Leading holistically also means living one's life motivated by a set of core values that place a high priority on integrity, service, and spiritual as well as monetary profit."[12] Integrity includes being absolutely candid and evidencing intellectual honesty in the things one says, consistency in dealing with others, honesty in handling conflict. It implies accepting what we have been and imagining what we can be. It is the spiritual discipline of always speaking the truth, of making sure we do what we claim we will do, and of being ready to hold on to the course of action. When a person has integrity he or she gains trust. However, the integrity must involve every aspect of one's life—personal, relational, organizational, and societal.

This basic leadership ingredient is an added value to competence. It is beyond expertise and motivation, it is the honesty that one's core beliefs guide one's decision making in leadership. It requires self-acceptance, truthfulness, fortitude, and inner peace. It establishes congruence between one's inner and outer reality. Individuals earn the right to be called leaders when people find authentic unity between their organizational and professional commitment and their spiritual lives. Kouzes and Posner offer six disciplines to support the credibility a leader's integrity earns: 1. Discover yourself, 2. Appreciate those you work with, 3. Affirm shared values, 4. Develop everyone's capacities, 5. Serve a clear purpose, and 6. Sustain hope.[13] In fact, a person is not free to lead unless he or she understands humanity, its nature, feelings, processes, and inner yearnings for self-actualization.

Leaders of integrity bring quality presence to all they do. Aware of their own stature as leaders, sensitive to their obligations to others in society, they can peacefully face the falsity and dark side of themselves, their communities, and society. Because of their integrity they can attain the characteristics of a successful leader, namely one who can challenge the process, inspire a shared vision, enable others to act, model the way, and encourage the heart of the followers.[14]

So, leaders of integrity are self-directed, proactive, always accountable, passionately committed to others, they take care of themselves, accept their own gifts, celebrate their own values and priorities, are candid with coworkers, and know what vision drives them. For such people, leadership is personal development—a journey from acknowledgment of our false selves to the acceptance of our own personal authenticity. It is also the context for individual and organizational development in which the integrity of the latter depends on the integrity of the former.

But they also internalize social responsibility, and are open to genuine dialogue with all around them, aware that their own experiences are always partial and fragmentary. They accept responsibility, blame no one, and prove every day that their moral centers influence all they do. Personal integrity and social responsibility must also conclude in institutional integrity. At a time when there are so many critics and pseudoexperts, a genuine leader stands up courageously for the institution he or she serves, constantly aware of the purpose of institutions and their normal tendency to self-corrupt. Endowed with courage of conviction, such leaders can move us beyond the comfort that institutions insist on providing, to the alternative ways of living as a community.

Personal, relational, institutional, and vocational integrity reinforce quality of life and lasting leadership. "Leadership lives at the intersection of the authentic and inauthentic, tilting the world toward the authentic. Leadership is always mindful that, as we call forth authenticity we can never forget that the conflicts and ambiguities of action reside not just in the world but also within ourselves."[15] Leadership is a spiritual journey to the depths of one's inner convictions, where, alone, one hears a call that no one else hears. Inner integrity calls leaders to be real, humane, open to the signs of the times, and confident in themselves and their values. On a more practical level it will require short response time, follow-up to problems, justification for decisions made, creativity, and willingness to be open to hidden opportunities. "These enduring leaders…know leadership is ultimately a spiritual journey of discovering and responding to each new challenge and question, with the abandon of 'yes' in the face of ambiguity, despair, and isolation."[16]

3. Results of Leadership with Integrity

Persons who are really in touch with themselves make the best leaders. They evidence dignity in their service of others and appear to others as having healthy self-esteem, socially satisfied, and fulfilled. They are known for their abiding sense of excellence, inner directedness, integrity, and commitment. These moral leaders are creators and stewards of core values; while always sensitive to the needs of followers, they above all stand tall for the values of the organization. They affirm, regenerate, and renew institutions. They freely choose their own identity, and it includes being known for integrity. Leaders of integrity are known for their clarity of mind and are people of breadth, never restricting their leadership.[17] They constantly foster trust, maintain open communication, and can let go of their own control to others. They are aware that their leadership has lasting value on their own lives, the quality of their work, the development of their community, and society in general. Such leaders gain stature among their peers, respect from superiors, even when they do not agree, admiration from people who do not share their views, and personal vocational fulfilment. Leaders who have integrity can handle conflict well for they are always willing to learn and always ready to treat others with understanding and compassion. They can relieve anger in a group by allowing discussion of the "undiscussible"; in fact, they can do the same with their opposition. Having worked hard for something and even been committed to it, they can also conclude with inner freedom and a nondefensive approach that "this reality is no longer acceptable."

Motivated by authenticity, ethical sensibility, and genuine spirituality, leaders of integrity are people of inner serenity and peace, resist being controlled, learn to skillfully neglect the petty or inauthentic values of their own organizations, find common ground with all kinds of groups, and can give comfort or create disturbance as appropriate. They love the institutions they lead and at the same time maintain a healthy skepticism toward them. Their authenticity and integrity lift the spirits of everyone and give hope to followers and community around them.

Followers give power and authority to people of integrity (referent power), they are proud of their organization, feel a genuine sense of ownership of it, and experience team spirit with the leader. Perhaps the greatest result in the lives of leaders of integrity is that they transform their institutions through ongoing conversion. Facilitating institutional conversion is a leader's primary task and is impossible without individual integrity. It needs to be clear to followers what the leader stands for and that he or she will be firmly dedicated to the mission and vision. "The evolution and development of a mature inner consciousness provide us with a resiliency, a joy, and optimism of life. This inner mastery enables us to assume the tasks of leadership by responsibly inspiring hope and confidence among others that the right path will emerge and we finally shall succeed."[18]

4. Building a Trusting Environment

Leadership is given to people of integrity by their followers who can just as easily withdraw it. Some pseudoleaders can try to achieve credibility by simply acting the part. Followers soon notice this. In fact, as we have seen, when a leader gives merely lip service to something, he or she gets lip service back from followers. Quality leadership is exercised within a trusting environment. Trust is the emotional glue that binds followers and leaders together. When a trusting environment exists, followers confidently rely on the authenticity of their leaders. However, a trusting environment also becomes the foundation for mutual respect, confident risk-taking, partnership, and collaboration. In a trusting environment both leaders and followers know that each respects the competence of the other, grants them freedom to act and even to make mistakes, identifies the blind spots throughout the organization, and will always highlight the positive wherever it is to be found. Failed organizations that lack trust still exist all over the world, riddled with control, rigidity, guilt, fear, intimidation, political infighting, suppression of dissent, and so on. These organizations are spiritually impoverished. Creating an environment of trust means eliminating fear of others' failures or competence, being able to live with ambiguity, always being ready to show flexibility, and appreciating the individuality of each one in the pursuit of a common goal. Creating a trusting environment requires a new set of virtues from leader and follower alike, as they will need to establish clear and practical institutional goals to maintain this working environment in which alone integrity can flourish.[19]

When a leader witnesses to a firm sense of inner and outer reality, opens up all lines of communication, and integrates all into the pursuit of the organization's goals, he or she binds the organization closer together. Followers recognize the leader's integrity and feel more intimately part of the organization, are increasingly proud of their organization, and manifest a greater sense of ownership of the organization and its shared vision.

6

LEADERSHIP AND REFLECTION

Leaders today must be men and women who can think, reflect, reintegrate, and transform the many aspects of their lives. Leadership is no longer based merely on knowledge, competence, and experience, unless these are linked with reflection that produces alternative ways of thinking and acting. In the past we tended to stress leaders who were doers and achievers, not reflective thinkers. Today's new models of leadership all demand critical reflection, imagination, and an openness to "the unknown, the unexpected, and the unexplored."[1] The source of real learning in one's leadership is within oneself, and each one must train himself or herself in the new skills needed to be a reflective person.[2] James A. Ritscher expresses this very well: "Overall, the process is one of calming the body and mind until intuitive wisdom comes through. Experience shows that the calmer we are, the more we have access to our creative and intuitive aspects. As we become calmer, we start to see dimensions of a problem we have never seen before."[3] Without reflection leaders cannot bring forth new ideas, and they lose the opportunity to refocus commitment.

This reflective leadership gradually becomes integral; the leader leaves nothing out, leaves no one out, leaves no one's opinion out, leaves no possibilities out. Likewise, this reflective leadership is nondiscriminatory but inclusive. "A transformational leader perceives in a more inclusive way. His/her vision extends to the inner depth of things. The light coming from the leader shines upon the object of inquiry and reveals its hidden pattern of being and becoming."[4] Thus, the reflective leader gets to the deeper underlying problems within an organization, as he or she confronts cognitive, emotional, and spiritual components of an issue. When leaders do not spend time in reflection, someone else always has to pay for it. It is useless asking a so-called leader to see a particular insight when he or she cannot see in ways that only reflection brings.

People who have been involved in leadership for some time can easily recognize that the best ideas do not come while immersed in stressful work but when one is thinking, reflecting, and at peace. The business of work is often the robber of inner peace. Leaders must create space, time, and attitudes that lead to reflective leadership. The first decade of the third millennium has witnessed many self-centered, greedy pseudoleaders whose lives lost the rootedness that a spiritual approach to life brings. In the years ahead the best leaders will be reflective—yes, prayerful; in fact, one becomes one's best self in action based on contemplative reflection. This is so true that one author can simply refer to "a contemplative leadership style."[5]

1. Leadership and Prerequisites for Reflection

Mature leaders have a healthy self-concept, maintained by an acquired sense of balance. Such leaders recognize their gifts and talents, accept their weaknesses, and nurture their skills for the service of others. They can resolve their own inner conflict, identifying and accepting both the negative by-products of their strengths and the potential for good in their weaknesses. These kinds of leaders make their own decisions, shape their own life, responsibly integrate themselves into society, and discern perspective on life.

Quality leaders are inspirational and have a passion for service. Their commitment is lived with energy, enthusiasm, and excitement. They sense responsibility for themselves, others, and society, can eliminate the sacred cows of their institutions, and have the courage to take risks.

Dedicated leaders are reflective and are always learners. They critically reflect on their own actions, listen to their own bodies and to others' input, and with environmental sensitivity listen to the world around them. They are always asking questions, are open to the Spirit, and embody prophetical challenges.

Great leaders are witnesses to the values they proclaim and are able to transcend themselves in their selfless service of others. People of empathy, benevolence, sensitivity, and compassion, they think with their hearts, as they struggle to discover consensus in others. They accept the transforming power of love and, with spiritual perception, seek the more and greater outside of themselves in the community.

The best leaders are people of inner peace who can integrate leisure into their lives. They have self-discipline, ability to manage others, and commitment to maintain balance in their lives between times of involvement and times of seclusion. They can live with anxiety and tension, concentrate on the task, and maintain healthy limits for effective work. Moreover, as people of balance their decisions and choices become self-defining.

Leaders are people who offer new horizons to their followers and move people beyond mediocrity and indifference. They give hope amidst the problems of contemporary working life. They are willing to take risks and transcend boundaries. As leaders they share their experience of the mystery of God and thus bring a sense of hope to followers, reestablishing the perspective of life under God, and providing the basis for value-oriented leadership.

Such leaders are able to do what they do because their lives are nourished by reflection and prayer.[6] In quiet reflection they discover their true selves, intensify a passion for service, humbly know they must always be open to learn, find their calling in self-transcendence, emphasize the need for balance in life, and move to the growth of a God-given future. Reflection nourishes and strengthens their lives.

2. Four Steps to Develop Reflection

The major preparations for reflective leadership can be viewed as one's personal contribution in attitudes of stillness, inspiration, concentration, and silence. Each of these is a gift and is also an acquired art that benefits both reflection and leadership. We need to specifically train ourselves in stillness of body. We need to sit still, do nothing, and completely relax. For people of religious faith, any of the present techniques for relaxation that help in the acquiring of stillness in the presence of God can be used. This first simple stage should not be passed over. In our present speed-prone age, it can be a real effort. In the long run, it pays high dividends. Linked to this outward relaxed position should be deep and regular breathing. The stillness that reflection and prayer require is also a fine attitude in daily life and leadership. People who are always rushing here and hurrying there are not noted for the quality of their presence to others, whether colleagues, family, or friends. No one can be consistently still in times of reflection, unless he or she can be still in the presence of others, giving them attention and interest. Stillness is not something that we can turn on for moments of reflection. Rather, it must be very gradually acquired through self-training and sacrifice. This effort to train oneself in stillness and to place oneself in the presence of God is a "prayer of the body."

To facilitate the second step in reflection one needs, throughout daily life, to train oneself in openness to the varied and continual inspirations of the day from wherever they come. To help the development of the genuine spirit of inspiration we need to know ourselves as we are, with the good and weak sides, and express ourselves as we truly feel. If we hide or close ourselves to the unacceptable about ourselves, this just becomes a block to our reflection and prayer. We also need to be open to being inspired by others and by the world; and here one need only apply the general principles of dialogue in openness to others and the signs of the times.

If in times of reflection and prayer and decision making in leadership we are able to show openness to inspiration, then it will be because we have developed in life this attitude of total attentiveness to the varied inspirations that come personally to us in our hearts, in others, in the world with its history, and in daily events. If we have not a listening heart and have not trained ourselves in the art of listening, then when a critical time of change and challenge comes it is humanly impossible for us just to switch on to becoming inspired or inspirational.

Thirdly, we must train ourselves to concentrate; then in dealing with others or in discerning institutional direction we will be able to concentrate individually and with others in the challenging moments of life. Here again, we have an act of reflection and prayer that is an art and we can develop it by the way we approach other aspects of our daily leadership life. Therefore, as a remote preparation for reflection and prayer, try to develop concentration. As Jack Hawley pointed out, "We discovered that when you search for the soul of any idea you have to enter into your own soul."[7]

The ability to concentrate, which is also a common necessity in human growth, is something to be acquired by daily effort. Only short moments are needed, a few minutes while traveling, a view in the city, a scene in the country, a person's face, a picture, a child—all can be objects of a moment's concentration. On the other hand, listening intensely for a short while to a piece of music, or just one sound, or a bird, or a person's voice, or the rustling of leaves—all can open us to concentrate on something we did not perceive before. This is the self-training and remote preparation we need for reflection and prayer and a preparation to discover the best in others.

The kernel of genuine reflection is silence, and of genuine prayer silence in God. There are several attitudes of daily life that can undoubtedly help and prepare the way for this recollected silence. Awareness of the quality of one's presence to others and recollection are fundamental. Effort given to this reflective silence is generally more profitable for growth in reflection than is anything else. To these ought to be added a cultivated sense of wonder and astonishment. These qualities are often missing in life today, but if reflective leadership must also include an attitude of openness to the ever newness of others and of organizational growth, we will need a genuine sense of mystery and wonder to appreciate what is always ahead of us, always new, and our growing efforts at concentration will be an aid here. In this connection we need a healthy sense of aloneness, an awareness of our own unfulfilment except through others and in God—in other words, the attitude of one who is a real searcher.

Above all, one needs patience and a willingness to wait. Sometimes in the reflective moments of a day we try to push ourselves—disliking emptiness, we return to the normal actions of each day at the first sign of "nothing happening." Those who do wait are generally the ones who can come up with a new insight, can see links with vision and mission, and can see how every member of the group "fits in." All these above attitudes are also aspects of daily life, and living through them in daily life can be a preparation for reflection and an enrichment of our leadership skills. Nancy Eggert suggests four means to enter into contemplative experience: 1. Through appreciation of the material world (appreciation). 2. By letting go and letting be (detachment). 3. Through creative breakthroughs (creativity). 4. By means of social justice and compassion (compassion).[8]

3. Qualities That Facilitate Reflection and Leadership

Leaders today need to be people of deep reflection, and we call such people contemplatives. Moreover, being a contemplative is a critical aspect of spiritual leadership. All Christians who wish to be great leaders can open themselves to the enrichment of contemplation. Others who wish to disassociate themselves from explicitly religious dimensions of life will need to involve themselves in practices similar to prayer and reflection even though they use nonreligious vocabulary to describe such activities and practices. Contemplation, however, does require approaches to life that are found in the broad sweep of values we have grouped under spiritual leadership. When these values are part of life, an individual will be a better contemplative and a better leader. Anyone who has worked in leadership knows that no action is complete until the leader and team have reflected on it.[9]

Contemplation requires stillness, quiet attentive waiting for values beyond ourselves (and for believers, for God). Growth is a gift, and believers do no more than prepare themselves to receive the gift. However, the attentive waiting is itself an effort that includes many factors that foster a contemplative experience. This is another way of looking at time. "The human core approach to time management is, first to know the difference between authentic and inauthentic experiences of time and, second, to achieve control over lived time."[10]

Contemplatives are persons who are comfortable with themselves, at ease with their own strengths and weaknesses, and yearn to identify who they are capable of being. At peace with themselves, they know authenticity is found in the center of oneself; not by having more or doing more but by being more. This inner peace produces creative and visionary leaders. "Meditation may help you achieve access to and control over inner space and inner time. To concentrate on them is also to expand your mind. As you get a sense of the infinity of your inner world, your mind will also expand its creative and innovative potential."[11]

Contemplatives are not afraid to be alone, isolated from others for a while. They do not need to fill every spare moment with activities. They are happy on their own, can enjoy prayer in solitude, and are aware of the enriching experiences of silence, emptiness, and stillness. Nowadays, leaders need to feel comfortable just facing critical decisions alone and being happy and peaceful about their responses. Once again, I quote from Koestenbaum: "Courage, like freedom, is the decision also for energy, the decision to be positive and enthusiastic, the decision not to be depressed, the choice to live with greatness. It is also the discovery of centeredness, the still point in your core that is the source of peace and thus of self-confidence and mature strength."[12] Time alone can also be an experience of self-emptying which precedes times of real fulfilment.

Contemplatives are people with a sense of purpose, free from distracting and disintegrating secondary values. Their lives are unified in one great commitment to the vision they pursue. They are detached from secondary attractions, or rather have integrated all dimensions of life into a single-minded, single-hearted dedication to their purpose in life. They are truly free people who are not controlled by selfish desires but are the pure of heart that the Beatitudes call happy. Speaking of individuals who experienced downsizing and grew through the process, Mary Pulley concludes: "The people who experienced transformative change all talked about tapping into something bigger than themselves that helped them through their transition process and put their job loss in perspective. They interpreted their experience as part of a bigger plan or a bigger picture."[13]

Contemplatives appreciate anything that is beautiful: people, senses, music, art, literature, or drama. The ability to experience something beautiful prepares for the best in others, the best in others' ideas, and for believers, the beautiful experience of God. The same is true of joy, as the contemplative enjoys life, friendships, and love, or food, drink, and entertainment. A person who can be enthusiastic about music or friendship can also possibly be enthusiastic about life, family, and work, and can enthuse others too. People who are rarely enthusiastic about life are unlikely to be enthusiastic about others, an organization's mission and goals, and so on. This includes a positive attitude to the world around us that enables us to be leaders who manifest a social responsibility for the environment around us. "Ecological virtues are habits that allow us to work lightly on this earth and therefore to pass on its blessings of health and wholeness, of goodness and beauty to future generations. Because we have been so oblivious of these virtues during the industrial era and the urbanization of our lives and souls in this century, it is important that we pay heed to them now."[14]

Contemplatives are skillful in finding opportunities to reflect, either spontaneously while out in the country, or parks, or by deliberately preparing a part of their home to be conducive to a reflective experience. Much of our contemporary world is distracting and disturbing, but a careful choice of place, artwork, colors, and music can foster the uplifting of spirit needed for genuine reflective prayer. Thus, Pulley suggests: "Learn how to learn by moving back and forth between the external and internal, combining action with reflection to derive lessons from experience."[15] Another author goes even further in linking the need for reflection with transformational leadership. "Meditation, contemplation, and reflection prepare the mind for wordless thought. Transformational leaders solve problems by not thinking about them, or perhaps we should say, by thinking about them without words."[16]

A contemplative experience cannot be fitted into a tight schedule but needs a prolonged, open-ended time. When many of us are trained to use time well, plan schedules, and use time management planners, it goes against the grain to leave adequate open-ended time for reflection, and yet it is necessary. When we begin to experience emptiness in times of reflection, it often seems appropriate to end, as if we have got the best out of that particular experience. However, the emptiness is frequently what is needed before a new phase with new alternative ideas emerges. Only when one is empty can one be filled with a new reality. "Awareness is not a giver of solace—it is just the opposite. It is a disturber and an awakener. Able leaders are usually sharply awake and reasonably disturbed. They are not seekers after solace. They have their own inner serenity."[17]

Contemplatives know the importance of the body for quality reflection and prayer. They take diet and exercise seriously and appreciate that the Christian tradition of fasting can have a healthy impact on a life that is reflective. With experience, each person finds an appropriate and comfortable posture, a position one can stay in for the prolonged period of reflection on values, ethics, mission, and so on. It is difficult to spend time in reflection if you are in an uncomfortable position, if your stomach is rumbling, or if you get a cramp. This prayer position of the body is an excellent preparation for contemplative reflection. A leader in tune with himself or herself can give self to others, to the organization, and to society.

Contemplation needs nourishing with ongoing education in values, complemented with good literature of all kinds and an awareness of contemporary world events. It is difficult to give quality leadership to others without ongoing education. Hitt indicates that he believes there are five types of knowledge that contemporary leaders need. "Knowing oneself, knowing the job, knowing the organization, knowing the business one is in, and knowing the world. Lacking any one of these sources of knowledge handicaps a leader."[18]

A basic conviction in this section of the book is that what is good for religious commitment is good for life in general and personal fulfilment in leadership for individuals. Reflection and prayer are further examples that faith and religion are never separate from human growth, since what is conducive to prayer growth is also part of a healthy recuperative experience, so suitable for today's busiest individuals.

4. Practices Supportive of Both Reflection and Leadership

The following are important prerequisites to contemplative reflection and also attitudes that are beneficial in reflective leadership: a sense of astonishment and wonder, concern for others, a sense of obligation, a healthy loneliness, an accepted experience of doubt and temptation, and finally a deep hope. Other necessary conditions include: faith exercised, common sense, and creativity. Perhaps we should not exclude the following prerequisites for contemplation: living faith, freedom of expression without inhibitions, and a life of communion.

These prerequisites for contemplation are also components of a leisured approach to life that nourishes our leadership. Those who give themselves to the service of others need a sense of wonder and mystery in the life chosen, a personal concern for all who share in the encounter, a sense of obligation toward individuals and community, a healthy acceptance of the loneliness that misunderstandings in dealing with others can bring, an accepted experience of doubt and temptation regarding the validity of aspects of this lifestyle, and finally hope. Likewise they need a living faith; freedom of expression toward others; and communion with all for support, friendship, and love.

I would like to suggest eight exercises that are preparatory to reflection. I also propose that these exercises are preparatory to a more leisured life for a busy leader. As reflection is not possible without them, or something like them, neither is leisure, and neither is leadership.

1. **Listening.** A helpful exercise to prepare for reflection is a self-training in listening, a quality that benefits our leadership. Close your eyes and pretend to be blind, receive all through your ears. Listen carefully for sounds outside the room, then inside the room. Do not hurry this but let it last for five minutes or more. This exercise can help in praying; it is also a vital quality for reflective leisure. Really listen to what others say. Block everything else out

and just listen. All other qualities added to relationships are wasted if listening is not the first.[19]

"Blessed are they who hear what you hear" (Matt 13:17).

2. **Seeing.** For quality reflection, focus on any one point or object. Any training like this is a training to concentrate on the decisions we encounter in leadership. When you look at a thing it changes you. Pay attention to the ordinary until you see what is of value. This prepares for the faith encounter of recollection; it takes time and restfulness. This seeing beyond the immediate picture helps leaders to get away from the tyranny of petty laws and the way things have always been done and to see something else. This self-training in listening also helps the leader to see and read a situation accurately.

"Blessed are the eyes that see what you see!" (Luke 10:23).

3. **Sitting Still and Doing Nothing.** A vital quality for reflection, this is also vital for a healthy leisured life. We need to resist the competitive consumer-society in which we live. We do not always have to show power, drive, insight. We do not always need to share, contribute, dialogue, discuss. So much of spirituality is permeated with compulsiveness. However, some of the greatest Christian qualities will always be important—abandonment, passive commitment to God, openness to divine providence. "Silence is the sound of creation. It is pregnant with life trying to be born. It is the great womb of creation. The transformational leader creates from this place."[20]

"Be still, and know that I am God!" (Ps 46:10)

4. **Relaxation.** Relax. Reflection cannot develop while the body is tense in all the muscles, and leadership is not possible without the rest that brings balance in life. Wellness and wholeness will not be developed amidst similar tensions of mind and heart reflected in the body. Relaxation

fosters inner peace and thus opposes the robbers of inner peace—frustration, fear, worry, anxiety, conflict, guilt, and ineffective adjustment strategies.

"But I have calmed and quieted my soul, like a weaned child with its mother; my soul is like the weaned child that is with me." (Ps 131:2)

5. **Development of the Other Senses of Taste, Smell, and Touch.** We all have touch hunger and anxiety. We all need to touch and to be touched. This surfaces also in our intense desire to be in contact with others, to share values with those around us. It surfaces in the need to have close personal relationships with the others who are significant in our life.

"Taste and see that the LORD is good." (Ps 34:8)

6. **Worship by Affirmation.** This and the next, are great aids to reflective leadership and help us develop benevolent attitudes in our leading of others. Look at a scene with concentration and from it rise to ultimate values and to God its maker. See anything in the scene of positive value, admire this, and affirm it to perfection. This training to focus on the positive has lots of practical consequences in leadership such as approaches to performance appraisal.

"Be perfect, therefore, as your heavenly Father is perfect." (Matt 5:48).

7. **Worship by Detachment.** As above, look and concentrate, but this time find what is not of ultimate worth and admire its opposite. Affirm the opposite and ask for the purification of the negative human quality. In this you should not become involved in the human negative, but immersed in the positive that is attainable. It helps us maintain distance from the negative we find in our organizational work. This practice can counteract the tendency among many leaders of selective perception—seeing only what they want to see.

This also gives courage to confront the falsity of the sacred cows of every organization—those things we think we can never be without.

"This teaching is difficult; who can accept it?" (John 6:60)

8. **Breathing Exercises.** This is a training in calmness for prayer and life. While developing calmness, it deepens our awareness of the care of the Lord for us, and our dependence on the Lord. One example of the many for Christians: breathe in with the prayer "The Lord is my shepherd." Breathe out with the prayer "therefore I lack nothing." The contemplative exercise and the conviction on ultimate values of life and love go together. This use of a mantra focuses our thoughts and reflection.

"The LORD God formed man from the dust of the ground, and breathed into his nostrils the breath of life." (Gen 2:7).

We have reflected on the links between reflection and leadership. What prepares us for the former can profoundly influence the latter. A great leader creates a sense of the spiritual within the organization. Most organizations today do not need plans and strategies, they need a healthy spirit that is life-appreciating and life-giving. For the spiritual leader leadership is not an occupation but a deliberate choice that permeates all life, physical, intellectual, emotional, and spiritual.[21]

7

SPIRITUAL LEADERS AND THEIR ORGANIZATIONS

1. Promoting Organizational Well-Being

We have seen the close connection between the quality of one's personal life, family life, working and organizational life, and social life. A leader brings together personal and vocational integrity, relational and family integrity, organizational and institutional integrity, and civic and public integrity. These commitments wax or wane together. We focus in this chapter on the importance of organizations modeling spiritual leadership. How many times have we heard that problems today are not in organizations, rather organizations are the problem? Among the important tasks of a leader we must include working with organizations, encouraging followers to always question and challenge institutions, and leading all to constantly change the organizations of which they are a part. Jaffe and his colleagues express this well when they say, "We cannot overcome the crisis facing organizations today unless we redefine the entire nature of the connection between individual and organization."[1] Individual workers are not means of production, passive and without initiative for the organization's future. Rather, people together are the organization and are coresponsible for its mission. A good leader will have a mission-centered approach to everyone, focusing on their core expertise, aware of their distinctive contribution, being a voice for the enduring value of each one's contribution, and living as the animator of a pervading passion for the attaining of shared goals. Marcic insists that what is needed is a fundamental transformation of organizational life that results in giving greater importance to justice, dignity, service, trust, and love.[2] Vail speaks of appreciating the spiritual nature of organizations and calls for a new paradigm of organizational life that offers "refreshing, even thrilling new interests in ethics, morality, and the spiritual nature of humanity, wherein a sense of process wisdom and the value of relationality will flourish."[3] Thus, we see in organizations these same values that when found in an individual lead to spiritual leadership.

People who wish to be leaders must have a compelling vision of what an organization can become. This will mean being honest about its current state and aware of what is really going on within the structure.[4] It will mean having a plan to renew and reinvigorate individuals in their roles, so that they can renew the structures. Such leaders are willing to work systematically at change, appreciate the need to involve the institute's central administration, and accept a slow process of a few years to give people the time they need to adapt. These leaders are aware that 15–20 percent will reject most of what they do—and will do it vocally, and probably no more than 30–35 percent will follow. Yet, the leader will have the courage to go on.

Leaders must promote organizational well-being, aware that centralized decision making on this issue will do little, but facilitating well-being in subgroups will eventually percolate up to the whole organization. Organizational well-being starts with assuring all employees of a healthy working environment characterized by mutual respect, trust, appreciation for each other's gifts, open communication, and shared values. A leader is not there simply to react to problems but to creatively bring an organization and its people to an exciting future of mature collaborative vision and mission. The leader is not only protector of the organization's spirit—for every organization has a spirit, good or bad, but the leader must nourish the spirit with new insight, adaptability, and new purpose, enrich it with the beliefs and spiritual energy of employees, manage it skillfully,[5] and constantly, prophetically challenge members to keep awake and alert to its values for today's society so that no one lapses into a comfortable passivity.

A leader seeks truth, shares love, and serves the common good, and promotes organizational well-being by creating an environment where people are not only valued for what they do but for who they are. No one can genuinely transform an organization unless they have learned how to transform themselves. Essentially this means thinking about and acting with people in ways that show more than trust and respect, in fact that show profound appreciation, love, and a sense of incompleteness without others. It means appreciating others' experiences, ideals, hopes, dreams, and struggles for wholeness and integrity.[6] These are leaders whose souls are filled with the profound spiritual values we have seen in previous chapters. Great leaders will implement these efforts on the well-being of an institution, extending them to the wider community, reaching out to family, community, and political communities too.

2. Empowering Individuals and Teams

Once a leader has resolved needs, proven insight, established vision, and opened others to the future, he or she should be ready to step aside and abandon his or her own direct leadership in favor of other new leaders coming forward. This is done through empowerment, by which the leader gives others the authority to act and thus leads others to lead themselves. Empowerment is more than allowing others to participate or even delegating certain responsibilities to others; it is a form of self-determination and self-efficacy.[7] In so far as it liberates others to lead themselves, it strengthens others' self-concept, gives them belief in their own abilities, and enables them to take responsibility for their own actions. It also motivates others to appreciate their roles in a common enterprise. Furthermore, empowering others means prolonging one's own leadership beyond one's departure or retirement. Empowerment deals with important issues, not the bogus empowerment that deals just with those issues that the leader does not want to bother with. Thus, empowerment includes vision statements, goal setting, decision making, establishing budget priorities, performance appraisal procedures, training, and evaluation. During empowerment the leader always maintains some guiding role since a leader can empower others with authority but can never let go of overall responsibility.

Great leaders see one of their most important tasks to be empowering others until they advance to the position in which they can serve the organization best of all. Gardner recommended a series of actions that would lead to empowering and enabling of others: sharing information, devolving initiative and responsibility, helping others attain their goals through their efforts, removing barriers to the release of others' energy, finding resources people need, resolving conflicts in the group, building appropriate structures to facilitate empowerment.[8] Randolph offers an empowerment plan in three stages: 1. Share information, 2. Create autonomy through structure, 3. Let teams become the hierarchy.[9] He then gives some excellent detailed components of each stage.

Whatever plan one follows, it should include at least the following. Empowering others begins by controlling the negative turbulence of an organization. Nothing significant is possible in organizational change when morale is bad, the rumor mill is overactive, or creative minds are absorbed in pseudo and unimplementable solutions to perceived problems. Then a leader should make sure that people who are ready for empowerment share the organization's basic values and culture. Empowering people who are not dedicated to the basic values will always end in chaos, although not every individual will be equally enthusiastic about every value.

As Randolph suggested, a basic requirement for empowerment is sharing information, including important information on goals and strategies, budget and profits, personnel strengths and weaknesses. A leader must promote open dialogue and the fostering of multiple perspectives on issues. Each person must know opinions are not received judgmentally, but are welcome. Through empowerment the leader should facilitate appropriate questions that themselves become part of improving the process. Thus, a leader asks, what are we each responsible for? Which issues would followers like supervisors to be more involved with? Which tasks do followers consider a waste of their time? Does what we do add any value to the organization or not?

Of course, a leader will need to establish new structures to find and release the power of participants because empowered people will be more motivated, self-managed, and self-evaluated. Empowerment does not happen by chance, but will need structures to train others, identify special skills, facilitate group discussion, prioritize goal setting, and so on. The leader must sustain efforts at empowerment by providing all teams with information, motivation, relational support, and both coordination and appreciation of everyone's efforts. A leader needs to be sure that followers truly have ownership of the organization's shared vision and goals. No one can be expected to dedicate themselves to goals they do not own, or to a vision and mission they never participated in establishing.

Along these lines followers should also be urged to set their own goals within the common ones, evaluate them, and redefine as needed. A leader will need to motivate followers' effectiveness through constant affirmation, redirection following failure, and ongoing self-assessment. A leader will encourage risk-taking among all those empowered to self-leadership. The lack of risk-taking can lead to serious damage to the organization's future as it becomes mired in doubt, hesitation, fear of the unknown, unwillingness to change, and so on. Linked to all stages of self-management the leader will emphasize self-criticism and individual, group, and mentor evaluation. However, evaluation should lead to resolving issues, problems, or failures together and/or letting followers resolve them themselves. Anyone involved in the empowerment of others should be ready to step aside when no longer needed, to celebrate the success of others, and to generate in followers pride in their accomplishments.

While empowerment can focus on everyone and on using the gifts of every individual for the benefit of the organization, a leader will take special care of creative people and the impact they can have on an organization. Leadership is not a function of a few charismatic individuals but a process dedicated leaders use to bring out the best in others. Most organizations invest in research and development, but many neglect the return on investment in the ideas, innovation, and creativity of dedicated members of the organization.[10] Creative people are always moving to something new and are never satisfied. Creative people are especially enriched in a workplace of diversity that can give rise to innovative ideas and nontraditional thinking. Leaders must provide ever new possibilities and be creative in facilitating the creativity of others.

Since creativity often implies struggle, leaders will need to be ready to accept more dynamic struggle than they would need to without creative people. Moreover, many workers today seek more satisfaction than that which comes from salary. They expect opportunities in flextime, dignity, vacations, and opportunities for creativity, among others. In fact, many workers look for working environments that let them be and become who they are capable of being. Fostering creativity means giving people time to think, innovate, share, rest, and explore without criticizing them for nonproductivity. This calls leaders to ask how they reward creativity or do they punish it, how they encourage independent thinking or do they expect conformity, how they facilitate open discussion opportunities or do they strictly control them.[11] Creative people are generally motivated to quality contributions to the organization by self-motivation rather than external motivation from rewards or punishment. Rather than being pushed by external stimuli they experience an internal pull to be faithful to their own values and integrity in work, to other people and visions they share, and even to world events and needs to which they feel called to respond.[12] They are people who exhibit not only professional commitment but discretionary commitment. Creative people make great contributions to an organization.

Empowerment should lead to the setting up of collaborative teams. Moreover, the best way to get people to work in teams is to give teams significant, fulfilling work to do. Teams are all over the place; many participate at low nonthreatening levels of organizational life. "Empowered teams are very different from participative teams, quality circles, or semi-autonomous teams. They make decisions, implement them, and are held accountable; they do not just recommend ideas."[13] Good leaders facilitate empowered teams in which members are dedicated to common values, shared purpose, mission, and strategic goals.

Leaders who empower such teams can stay in the background but cannot disappear from the scene. They will need to guide the team through its own stages of development.[14] Wilson and colleagues refer to three stages:[15] 1. The pre-team phase when the leader needs to help people overcome their resistance, buy into the concept, lay aside their fears, and start the changes necessary to become a team. 2. The new-team phase can last about eighteen months during which time the leader needs to make sure there are adequate challenges in significant work and that each team member identifies his or her role. At this time the team will need to work on establishing common basic values, shared purpose, team mission, and goals. 3. The mature phase of implementation of the team concept requires courage on the part of the leader to step aside and let the team become self-managed, even to the point of managing its own crises. At the same time a leader must protect the autonomy of the team from the fears of higher executives. Empowerment can lead to out-standing development and to opportunities for new discoveries. There are few failed leaders worse than a narcissistic leader who fears to facilitate the growth of others and stunts the life of the organization.

3. Signs of an Organization Directed by a Spiritual Leader

The leadership style of an organization directed by a spiri-tual leader would be *collegial government* in which a leader discov-ers his or her true self in the group or community with which he or she works. This requires the humility to realize a leader does not have all the answers, and the awareness that genuine organi-zational direction percolates up to the leader from followers.

The organization is *led by mission and values,* not by organi-zational goals and objectives. It is shared mission, values, and vision that enthuse and motivate the organization. However, these underlying core values and sense of shared destiny develop, and, yes, change, with the input and experiences of all members. Mission, values, and vision do not tell us about the organization's origins, but how it sees itself today and tomorrow.

In this kind of an organization with collegiality as the gov-ernmental model the *administration is collaborative* at all levels in the structure. Collaboration takes place on three different levels, intellectual, organizational, and personal, and includes an appreciation of how each person contributes to the common goals of the organization.

In this kind of organization decisions are made at the lowest level in the structure. This *commitment to subsidiarity* pushes authority down and refuses to allow gifted members to remain empty and feel less valued while decision making is reserved to executives who do not need to be involved. These organizations are self-generating, healing, and liberating.

A spiritual leader's organization channels effectiveness and achievement to *self-managed teams* in which members are self-directed. This is the foundational experience of the organization's purpose and effectiveness. The organization's identity is strong here or nowhere. Team members inspire each other, motivate each other, and foster mutual growth. Members of self-managed teams develop new behaviors and new ways of thinking that percolate up and influence the whole structure.

Such an organization gives importance to *building community* and welcomes everyone as important contributors both to work and to community life. In a healthy organization relationships contribute to each one's health and self-esteem, and highlight the human values of compassion, empathy, love, and friendship. Such an organization fosters community through its own rituals, stories, symbols, and celebrations.

This kind of organization manifests *special appreciation for its workers,* not only in matters of work environment, salary, benefits, and morale, but also in fostering a mind-set of consultation, listening, getting feedback, and a commitment to diversity.

Every organization moved by inner values develops *a culture of openness and trust.* Communication is very important and channels of communication are carefully maintained. This approach includes open records whenever possible, including financial documents, executives' salaries and benefits, trustee actions, and so on. This free flow of information generates trust and a sense of belonging.

A spiritual leader fosters in his or her organization a *dedication to ongoing education.* This starts in the hiring process, and leaders continue it in carefully planned training, and it is maintained through the freedom to learn and experiment both with products or services and with internal organizational life. This dedication to ongoing education includes meaningful dialogue, sharing of ideas, questioning assumptions, debating company strategies.

4. Stages of Growth in an Organization Led by a Spiritual Leader

Generally, people partially identify with an organization's core values and mission. There is nothing wrong with this; in fact it leads to a healthy tension that keeps individuals focused on constantly challenging each other and the organization's direction. A lot of time and effort precede the organization's commitment to leadership based on spiritual values. Sofield speaks about four stages that lead up to a common dedication to implement a collaborative approach to life.[16] Adapting his four stages to the preliminaries to an organization motivated by spiritual leadership we see that stage one is when people in the organization simply presume that they already are dedicated to the common vision, but in fact they do little to show it, and the proof that they are not committed is that the organization remains rigidly hierarchical. Stage two in remote preparation is when a group is obsessed with their approach to leadership; they are constantly talking about it and circulating documents and holding workshops, but the proof that there is no real dedication is that the endless discussion never leads to action. The third stage in preparation is when the group is characterized by ambivalence; they believe in the values of spiritual leadership but this is coupled with fear and anxiety, some resistance and even anger. The sign of this stage is that there are efforts to implement leadership values but no long-term commitment. The fourth stage is one of action, when commitment to spiritual leadership becomes an institutional norm and people work to implement the vision even when it is difficult. Put simply, before people arrive at a willingness to dedicate themselves to a shared vision of leadership they must pass through four phases: "we should do it," "we want to do it," "we can do it," and finally "we will do it." Needless to say, some organizations do not make this decision, and there may even come a time when it is best to let an organization die. Keeping institutions on life-support is a disservice to everyone involved.

Once members of an organization have passed through the remote preparations and have reached the point of wanting to become an organization based on spiritual leadership, then the group takes on a life of its own. Leaders need to remember that groups that share deeply are generally from about eight to ten participants, and in some cases with less profound sharing it is possible to work with groups up to about thirty-five members. In large organizations leaders need to work with participants with awareness that the organization is a community of smaller communities. There are three essential elements for the life of any group: relationships, common task, and the interaction between these two. When only the first is present you have a group of friends, when only the second you have a work group with no interpersonal interests, but when you have interaction between relationships and common task—a simultaneous growth of friendship and efficacy of work, then you have the beginnings of common commitment and shared values.

Members dedicate themselves to a group's purpose because they believe they will benefit from it. No group becomes an organization motivated by spiritual values because the boss wants it. Rather members believe they have something to give and receive on the level of task and on the level of life. People are motivated initially by their own psychological needs and commit themselves to organizational goals because they feel it gives them opportunity to fulfil their personal aspirations, frees them from their own isolation, gives them social significance in interaction with others, leads them to personal fulfilment, allows them to express their own originality, gives them the chance to be someone and to succeed, and because they sense there is proportion between the efforts needed and the results expected. A wise leader will always keep these needs and hopes of members well focused, and realize that if they are not answered there will be no quality organizational growth.

Once the remote preparatory stages have passed and the leader who continues to guide the group is well aware of the members' hopes and needs, then the move toward becoming a value-based organization has five stages. No one can impose a prefabricated scheme on others, but must start from concrete situations of individuals' basic values. Any group or organization like individuals moves through stages of growth and decline, radical breakthroughs or organizational death. For some writers, the transformation "is so dramatic that organizations must experience 'metanoia,' or fundamental change. If organizations fail to become metanoic organizations, they cease to compete."[17]

Five Stages in the Growth of an Organization Led by a Spiritual Leader

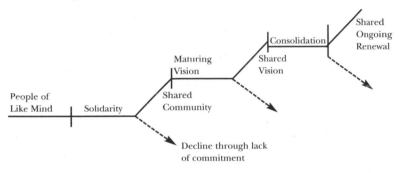

Stage 1	Stage 2	Stage 3	Stage 4	Stage 5
Gathering Like-Minded	Solidarity through Shared Community	Maturity through Shared Vision	Consolidation	Ongoing Renewal

Stage One—A Meeting with Others of Like Mind

Why should people come together to focus on a shared vision? It starts in a concrete situation of daily working life. It is just a simple fact that takes on profoundly human significance when several people realize that they share the same intuitive vision of what the group can become. While this stage can come about by chance or be the result of a common experience, such as a group of workers participating in the same workshop, it is generally the fruit of a leader's enthusiasm, inspiration, and skillful articulation. The leader's first challenge is that the group become a community that unifies both their life and action. In this early stage the leader exercises a teaching role, a community-building role, and a discerning role of discovering how each member can become an integral part of this group.

Stage Two—Building Solidarity

This is a time of reflection and discussion on what it means to be a value-based organization. Clearly the task takes prime importance, for the work needs to continue, but there is also increasing interest in how the work is done, how the organization functions, and what the role of each member should be. It is a time of sharing of values and friendship, an increasing appreciation of the group but also of oneself and one's own role in the group.[18] It is a time of community building. People become aware of the balance between real belonging or identification and a genuine sense of self-direction, or between the ability to collaborate and an ability to live out one's own role. It becomes clear that building solidarity in organizational life does not mean absorption or conformism, but rather personal discovery and organizational vision can go together. However, stage two ends in a crisis, generally based on the fact that some members feel that this common commitment and struggle for a shared vision is too demanding. Some feel the weight of new demands and see that they must personally change. They came to the organization for a job, not for a community of solidarity in shared values and vision. So at this time several individuals will begin to withdraw. This resistance can intensify, and a leader must be able to manage this resistance carefully. It is a period of pain and tension that is overcome with a breakthrough experience in which people become aware that the true direction of their personal lives is intimately linked to the kind of life they live in organizations. It is another experience that leadership is who you are and not just what you do.

Stage Three—Maturing the Shared Vision

During this period it is the job of the leader to animate and coordinate the group's efforts to implement the vision of leadership. The leader must be a model of spiritual leadership, leading the group to a discovery of appropriate mission values, goals, and strategies. The leader can show that this vision is centralized and decentralized at the same time. This shared vision has been with the group for some time, but now the group needs to develop common strategies of leadership to achieve the common vision. In achieving this together the group comes up against the ways of doing things of each one, and this leads to further tensions and a second crisis. This second crisis is more painful than the first because the members' ties are now deeper. It can also be the time of divisions within the group because the rhythms of maturing are different, and at this time many will pull back and some will leave the organization. This can also be a time when others surface in the group to lead the group in different ways, and the original inspiring leader may feel threatened, but should not abandon the shared vision. During this struggle the leader makes his or her own spiritual commitment in the experiences of adversity.

Stage Four—Consolidating the Vision of an Organization

The crisis at the end of stage three is again a breakthrough to a mature commitment to be a spiritually motivated organization and to an appreciation that this will impact every aspect of organizational life. Donna Markham expresses well some of the effort that typifies this period. "Spiritlinking—the deliberate and untiring act of working through resistance to organizational transformation by building the circle of friends, fostering networks of human compassion and interweaving teams of relationships through which new ideas are born and new ways of responding to the mission take form and find expression."[19] This is a period of internal organizational consolidation and at the same time a period of fruitful action on the surrounding community, other organizations, and society. Complex institutions that develop successful structures can become powerful motivators of other institutions—helping them to become models of community, healing, and service. I have always insisted that leadership is personal, relational, organizational, and societal. This is the time when what is learned in an organization impacts all aspects of a person's life. This is also a period when the organization becomes increasingly aware of the contributions of all in the group, whether inspirers, visionaries, organizers, doers, planners, evaluators.

Stage Five—Renewal

During this final stage the group focuses on three things—action, evaluation, and training. Action without training degenerates into superficial activism; action and training are not achieved without evaluation; and evaluation without ongoing training becomes superficial. This stage includes communal evaluation of the group's life and progress; evaluating, renewing, and reinterpreting values that may have lost their focus. This is a time to again liberate the energies of everyone in the group, to reenergize participation in the establishing and achieving of common goals, and to focus on a renewed enthusiasm and commitment to the shared vision and mission. This is the third and final breakthrough experience that gives life to the group.[20]

5. Structural Components of an Organization Led by a Spiritual Leader

Members of an organization know who they are and who they want to be. Leaders of such organizations, even though gradually taking a back seat, must continue to motivate, sustain, encourage, and challenge the organization in fidelity to its shared vision. Leaders and members alike will make sure that the organization has a series of components of its life that enable its values to be sustained. Key among these are the four core components: a values statement, a shared vision, a mission statement, and a strategic plan. Underpinning these core components are four useful tools to sustain the shared values: an executive group, a team charter, a code of ethics, and an oversight board. Finally, there are four useful additional procedures that facilitate organizational development: hiring procedures, decision-making procedures, conflict-management procedures, and due process for resolution of grievances. These varied components of organizational life contribute to decentralizing decision making, simplifying processes, and furthering interdisciplinary team values.

A *values statement* is chronologically the first item in working toward shared vision. It refers to what drives individuals; what are the core spiritual principles that move a person in life. These values refer to what people basically stand for, and what they believe in. Since these will often be different for different people, a group must work toward a values statement that all the members of an organization can share. There is no mission or vision that is not based on shared values, unless it is imposed on others by a leader who has an exaggerated opinion of himself or herself. Jaffe and colleagues propose seven steps in crafting a team values statement—seek key values, share key values, rank key values, discuss gaps in the values, determine neglected or unexpressed values, create a group Credo, and then align behaviors with the values.[21] Once a group arrives at consensus on values the rest of the corporate life can develop. The Credo can then become a reference point for further discussion on the essential direction of organizational life. It will, of course, evolve and move through several transitional correctives that will help to refocus the group's dedication.

Every organization needs to formulate what its basic purpose is. This shared vision of how people in the organization see themselves grows out of the values statement. It is answering the questions who we are and what we can do that no one else can do. This *shared vision statement* articulates corporate self-understanding and guides all further decisions on organizational identity. Leaders cannot presume there is a vision, nor will the vision be identical in two organizations within the same corporation, even though there will be common ground. You do not have a vision to start with, but it emerges through consensus in the group.

A *mission statement* flows from the members' shared philosophy of life. "Mission" comes from a Latin word meaning "sent," and a mission statement expresses what a group thinks it has been sent into this world to accomplish. So, this is the articulation of organizational destiny. It will need to be clear, challenging, at once understandable by all in the organization but powerful enough to motivate and enthuse. A mission statement represents a communal commitment to what an institution wishes to be. Once it is formulated, everyone should be able to see themselves in it, and immediately appreciate both the challenge and opportunities it offers.

Finally, among the core components is *a strategic plan* that incorporates specific goals over one or several years, which arise from the shared values, vision, and mission. When dealing with a strategic plan—the values, vision, and mission are condensed into a group of long-range objectives, each objective is gradually attained by means of a series of goals, and each goal is achieved by a set of strategies. The strategies must specifically answer who will do the task, when, how, with what resources, and so on.

Underpinning these core components are four useful means to implement the shared values. First, there is an executive group of top leaders whose responsibility it is to make the day-to-day decisions within the organization. Emphasis on teams, consultation, and collaboration never removes the need for executive leadership. Even self-managed teams leave much to *a leadership team*. Broad-based input and consultation never deal with more than 20 percent of decisions in organizational life. People have a job to do and both need and want to get it done. If an executive team is reliable in matters pertaining to the essential commitments of an organization, everyone else will leave them alone to run it.

Within the organization and under the leadership of an executive group, teams become the basic structure of the organization, and they do well to establish a team charter of agreed components of their own organizational life. Jaffe and colleagues suggest that *a team charter* should express members' agreement on seven aspects of their communal life—purpose, tasks, boundaries of authority, measures to determine success, required training for membership, group rules of behavior among team members, and team meeting requirements.[22] Each of these can be expressed simply while establishing boundaries that assure peaceful agreement and common expectations.

All members of an organization should agree to *a code of ethics*. A code of ethics is a consequence of a mission statement and embodies common ethical commitments that must be lived by anyone who accepts a shared mission. It should not be imposed on followers but ought to be the result of everyone's input so that everyone will have ownership. It presumes ongoing education in ethics issues that are relevant to the organization in question and will most likely require an ethics committee to oversee the drafting of the code, its implementation, and its adaptation to new situations. A code of ethics needs to be valued by everyone in the organization, but especially by decision makers who can make it obvious to followers that ethics form an integral part of the decision-making process.

Some people find codes of ethics unnecessary either because they seem to be laws imposed on everyone rather than action that results from principle-centered convictions, or because they find unacceptable suggestions that there needs to be separate ethics for particular organizations or professions, rather than the common principle-based ethics of good men and women. However, codes of ethics do manifest a common recognition of consequences of a shared mission, they help in the ongoing education of members of an organization, they show others the organization's common commitment, and they manifest the priorities of the organization.[23]

Finally, a useful structure to underpin and support an organization's commitment to its shared values is *an oversight board* made up of respected men and women who appreciate the organization's dedication to the shared values of leadership and can become both a sounding board and an outside evaluation board for the successful implementation of values. This should not be the old-fashioned trustee group made up of individuals who have money and know how to get more. Rather this group should be individuals who know the mission values and can see when they are implemented. Annual or quarterly meetings can be opportunities for the organization to articulate to others the developments it is making and receive input and challenge on its fidelity to its own stated goals.

The spiritual leader's organization should utilize well four procedures as aids in the implementing of its vision and self-understanding. First, *hiring procedures*, while respectful of legal requirements, will be very clear regarding the corporate culture into which a person is asking to be hired. There is no obligation to hire someone who does not share the organization's basic values, vision, and goals. The hiring procedure is the first stage in the training of new members, and applicants should be introduced carefully and deliberately to the value system that is part of the job. The job announcement, interview process, organizational documents, team encounters, and top leaders' articulation of common commitments should all focus on the job at hand and the way, and with what spirit, that job is done in this organization.

In any organization it is useful to have a clear understanding of *decision-making procedures*. What kind of decision will call forth what kind of involvement by members? Clearly decisions that required extensive input in the formulation of values, vision, mission, and goals cannot be changed except by similar involvement. The arrival of new executives for leadership roles should have no immediate impact on shared vision. The newcomer must become a member of the community before getting involved with critical issues. Vision is not the CEO's but belongs to the community. A simple rule of thumb is that everyone influenced by a decision should participate in the process.

Mature organizations know that conflict is part of life; it need not be viewed negatively. In fact, it can be an opportunity to involve all who are involved in the conflict and facilitate a deeper appreciation of each other and of the issues. Leaders also appreciate that conflict left unaddressed gnaws at an organization and becomes resistance to change. *Conflict-management procedures* can clear the air and help the group work toward constructive solutions that are a sign of organizational vitality. Members of a team can identify major causes of conflict for them—are they people, situations, attitudes, or topics? Some individuals or groups deal with conflict in a win/lose style, achieving solutions but damaging relationships. Others have an accommodating style, preserving the relationships but achieving nothing. Others use an avoidance style—they "turn off," or just leave the discussion. Some others have a compromise style in which both sides yield a little but no one is fully satisfied. Finally, some strive for a win/win style which gives consideration to all involved and yet focuses on those whose emotional reactions seem to be the source of the problem.[24] In healthy conflict management there is a good relationship between the parties, each accepts conflict as part of growth, each is willing to be involved and to change, each deals with real facts and never another's motives, and the issue is dealt with briefly, resolved, and both sides move on, forgetting the past, accepting the consequences of conflict, and bearing no grudges.

Finally, organizations need well-established and publicly known *procedures for the resolution of grievances*. Generally, this will include several stages, beginning with discussion with the team leader and possibly ending in legal action. Following discussion with the team leader, if dissatisfaction continues and no resolution emerges, gradually the grievance can be appealed to higher levels of organizational life. Leaders do not need to agree with the grievance but they can be thoroughly respectful in making sure procedures are known and followed carefully and speedily. Outcomes cannot be guaranteed but respect for all involved and good use of the procedures can be. In fact, whether dealing with conflict or grievances, the transformational leader can use the procedures to bring opposing parties together. "By finding the 'middle way,' the energies of both parties are synthesized into new organizational creations. The secret is to balance the energies, not exhaust them by playing them against each other."[25]

Conclusion

There are no leaders outside group development and no transformational leaders outside collaborative structures. Leaders must help followers change themselves into leaders. Organizations based on spiritual values are the result of leaders transforming the structures of which they are a part. Not everyone will agree with this development, some will follow, others will leave, and still others will remain but become polarized. Over a period of time the institutional vision self-selects followers and the organization consolidates its shared values. As individual leaders must not reduce the ideal of their calling, neither should organizations. Eventually, this kind of organization becomes a model for other organizations and can maintain its focus with even a 30 percent turnover of personnel. Once an organization commits itself to implement the vision of spiritual leadership, the journey begins and all members will need to be constantly alert to maintaining the vision they have together chosen. Renewal will need to become ongoing.

8

SPIRITUALITY OF LEADERSHIP

Introduction

Often in the last decade or so writers have used the term *spirituality* to describe the package of values that together enable a person to exercise spiritual leadership if embraced consistently. So, the starting point, an experience of "faith," becomes a blueprint of life. This lifestyle that results from "faith" is what we call "spirituality," and that part of spirituality that interacts with or is implemented in times of leadership is what we call "spiritual leadership." The values implemented in spiritual leadership will be no different than those implemented at home with one's spouse or children, in social and political life with colleagues and friends—it is just the context that is different. "Spirituality is beyond us, and yet it is in everything we do. It is extraordinary, and yet is extraordinarily simple."[1] Several writers refer to the ever-widening range of a leader's influence. Dorothy Marcic addresses the possible growth of love and spirituality at different organization levels. She asks four questions: what do love and spirituality look like, what helps develop love and spirituality, what blocks love and spirituality, and what are loving and spiritual outcomes? She then applies questions to four aspects of a leader's life: individual, team, organization, and society,[2] thereby confirming the expansiveness of a spiritual dedication.

1. Christian Spirituality—Its Focus and Components

In this section we look at the nature and components of spirituality. In the last decade many writers have presented entire chapters on spirituality without ever indicating what it is. Spirituality never refers to static concepts but only to dynamic ones. It is not interested in prayer but growth in prayer, not charity but growth in charity, not social justice but growth in one's commitment to social justice. Spirituality refers to the development of a life based on values, and Christian spirituality refers to the development of a life that is centered on the values proposed by Christ. It implies the total integral development of the individual, social, and cosmic dimensions of life, as a person directs the evolution of the whole of life on the basis of these core values. Faithful following of a call from God in Christ leads a person to find self-fulfilment, and to a dedication that makes a qualitative difference in the way people behave in their daily lives, giving them values, vision, purpose, and perspective on life. Christian spirituality brings life and growth into authentic focus as it highlights the genuine concerns of life and human hope. It opens the way to the fullest and deepest values of human growth, the profound and intimate values we cherish most: the yearning for self-fulfilment, for community, and for transcendence. A business professional who is motivated by "faith" brings all this with him or her when coming to work and hopes that work too will play a significant role in a longing for fullness of life with God.

Christian spirituality stresses the means and methods that facilitate development in life, and identifies the elements and causes of growth. It can offer to others a strategy for their own growth while appreciating that each individual's way to human-Christian maturity may well be different than the recognized standards of any time or place. Rooted in the message of Jesus, interpreted and applied in light of one's own and others' experience, Christian spirituality studies the growth of the person from God's perspective—and presupposes all facets of our knowledge of humanity. Spirituality is more than a segment of life, a Sunday addition; it is a way of viewing the whole of life.

Having as the goal of spiritual development the attaining of mature Christian life, believers claim this end is realized in many varied and original ways, depending on the conditions of individuals and the free action of the Holy Spirit. Christian spirituality aims to integrate the unique message of Jesus with the best of all human values and produces a living synthesis of divine call and human response as they can be found in mature adult personalities.

Spirituality used to be more systematized, emphasizing method, formalism, analysis, and individual needs, as can be seen in some of the spiritual movements of history. Contemporary spirituality concerns itself with the concrete circumstances of our own age, and stresses spontaneity, personal authenticity, global vision, and vital needs. Recent spiritual renewal focuses on a rediscovery of the essential source values of faith and an opening to the autonomous values of the world. These discoveries have led to a simplification of spiritual life and a fundamentally positive attitude to the world. This has also led to new ways of thinking and living Christianity that imply a new value for human and earthly realities, an awareness of personal responsibility for others, and a new community consciousness in believers. Thus, it impacts directly our leadership style.

Spirituality for a person of faith is the interaction of God's gift of transforming life with the efforts of the believer in concrete circumstances of history. Thus, it is always *a transitory manifestation of perennial values*. Rooted in the great tradition of Christ's message, it cannot degenerate into religious fads while neglecting essential values of faith. Each believer, faced with his or her own emptiness, needs to be open to grace and to develop the faithfilled skill of waiting for God's interventions, together with an attitude of readiness to receive God's gifts and use them creatively.

Christian spirituality presumes *a positive approach to creation,* whether that be the world around us or our human nature created and redeemed by God. Spirituality now refers to the concrete daily living of those Christians who deliberately try to make their faith real and effective on a day-to-day basis. This trend stresses the importance of faith-motivated professional life.

Spirituality is *faith brought to birth in ever-changing circumstances of modern life*. Faith allows God's power to be fruitful in us. Spirituality is directly connected with human nature, making it what it is capable of being. It grows principally by purifying, directing, and enriching that life and not by sacrificing it or escaping it. Therefore a Christlike approach to social and political involvement is preferable to withdrawal; a striving for economic justice and a sharing of poverty and wealth are more significant than an artificial poverty in the midst of security; the effort of building a chaste and loving family and sexual life is more important than their absence.

Spirituality is *rooted in a faith experience,* in this case in Christ and the common search to bring about the coming of the kingdom he announced. While the implementing of the reign of God needs to be conducted with a constant healthy skepticism toward the artificial claims of institutionalized religion, the search for the values of the reign of God should always take precedence over organized religion. Jesus' own struggles against organized religion in his day led to opposition and eventual death. Likewise contemporary spirituality always implies the acceptance of suffering and sacrifice as a response to this world's selfish leaders— those who need power and cannot share it, who must oppress others to remain in control, who expect to be supported by the poor, who fear peace and the threats they think it brings to them. Mary Pulley speaks of faith-filled people who make sense of their experiences when she says, "Faith provides a deep resting place for the heart. Having faith in ourselves means resting in the confidence that we will know how to respond to whatever comes our way. We can do so with hope and imagination."[3]

Spiritual development occurs only with others. Autocrats, lonely "prophets," modern messiahs, ecclesiastical totalitarians, deluded grand evangelists, and charismatics are not candidates for the common search for life in God, no more than they who selfishly pursue their own satisfaction and betterment. They who cannot share life or the service of others, or who cannot cooperate or collaborate, or who cannot celebrate together or build community together—are at an enormous disadvantage from a Christian point of view. Rather, genuine growth includes a letting go of selfishness toward others and self-pity toward oneself, and it calls for confident and courageous growth with others. Spirituality is directed to others in the essential Christian characteristic of service. The interaction with others is a way of embodying spirituality, and at the same time the interaction with others in mutual service creates and constitutes the spirituality.

Spirituality is a manifestation of reality. It is the way in which people can become their true selves in response to God's call, and therefore it cannot coexist with any kind of escapism. It must be lived by individuals responding to their lives and destiny with God. This will imply constant creativity rather than any acceptance of prepackaged and recycled spirituality, whether in the form of saints from the past or spiritual movements of more recent times. For each of us God's call in the Lord is to become who we are truly capable of being. Thus, spirituality touches the masculine and feminine in each of us, never turning the values of either into an unacceptable enemy, as happened in some spiritual tendencies in the past. Rather we must reclaim both aspects and integrate them into an evolving self-awareness.

Spirituality is creative fulfilment, not a battle against embodiment, and is only achieved through our embodied lives. Christianity does not morbidly focus on suffering and death but on growth and new life (Eph 4:24). Expressing our inner feelings through our bodies and rarely without them, our faith- and hope-filled love appears in a smile, touch, embrace, compassionate glance, weeping. Spirituality is not the discovery of my inner, spiritual, supernatural self, but the directing to God of the whole of life. It optimistically stresses growth rather than a narcissistic focusing on one's own asceticism and spiritual needs. Spirituality includes an appreciation of the basic value of Christian poverty—that true simplicity of life that leads to a single-minded dedication to God and to nothing else that is not integrated into the God-directed nature of our lives. This just and holy attitude toward things, Scripture's purity of heart, influences our entire faith-filled approach to life. The Christian Scripture proclaims the importance of poverty in spirit (Matt 5:3), but is really asking that we be "poor with spirit."

Spirituality includes an ecological dimension through which the believer appreciates and enjoys the environment, learns from its balance and interdependence, and accepts his or her role in it. The believer can see the environment as his or her teacher of the strengths and weaknesses of earthiness and creatureliness. A sympathetic understanding of the ecosystem teaches the believer that spirituality includes a healthy approach to one's own physical life both by positively developing one's physical life and by accepting the hardships of life. The former includes fostering the body's health and well-being through diet, exercise, sports, leisure, and the development of one's sexuality. The latter capitalizes on Christianity's tradition of assuming sickness, pain, and all physical problems into a self-purification and attitudinal enrichment in union with the sufferings of the Lord.

Spirituality is a life of reflection and prayer. Prayer is a way of describing our God-directed lives. Growth in the spiritual life, seen as the life of prayer, is slow, and includes efforts to purify self, others, and the world of sin; to face reality as it is, drawing fullness out of the present moment; to deepen our appreciation of everyone and willingness to listen to all; to be open to every new dimension of our experience of God; and to root and celebrate our prayer in the worship of a loving community.

So, spirituality refers to the growth and evolution of life based on motivating values. It is a transitory manifestation of unchanging values. It implies a positive approach to all aspects of creation. It is the experience of faith brought to birth in the decisions of daily life. Spiritual growth occurs only with others, with a sense of reality and creative fulfilment, and with a positive attitude to ecology. It can be seen as a reflective life that is often called prayer.

2. Christian Spirituality and Spiritual Leadership

One of the major developments in the last couple of decades has been an extraordinary interest in integrating faith and professional activity. *Spirituality permeates one's commitment to every aspect of life.* This results from people realizing that all life including their family and working lives with their new focuses of call is always a reliving of the baptismal challenge to belong to Christ, to live and love for him. This leads us to relate differently to self, others, and even the cosmos because of a new way of living our relationship to Jesus. The service of others in professional life is a particularly splendid way of realizing this. This call will need to be renewed on a daily basis, as believers face increasing demands that must never lead to a reduced ideal of their calling.

Both feeling called by faith and yearning for personal integration Christian leaders strive to respond each day to the implications of that call they feel deep in their hearts.

Spirituality includes a sense of humility, the humble awareness that Christians are not born as such, but struggle daily to become what they hear the Lord calling them to be. No period can pass without learning something new either in prayer, in sharing with peers, in ongoing study, in reflective application of the word of God, in discussion with other believers, in the varied forms of openness to the many doers, thinkers, or teachers among us. Always aware of their own human frailty, Christians will value a sense of humility, knowing that leadership brings its own brands of pride, arrogance, and abuse of the power that was given to serve others.

Spirituality is rooted in the life of Christ and can frequently be accessed through the formulations of belief and religion, so a leader who wishes to emphasize those core values of Christ must include ongoing knowledge of the message and skills to interpret it in professional life. The former includes the knowledge of the sources of the faith. The latter develops areas of contemporary knowledge that can enlighten spirituality, such as psychology, sociology, anthropology, and so on. Moreover, it includes leadership training, communication skills, religious education methods, a knowledge of group processes, and ability to direct other disciples in their pursuit of encounter with God.

A spiritual leader's spirituality stresses *an appreciation of institutions with their awkwardness and graciousness.* Sometimes the spiritual leader will have to denounce the negative in institutions, even in religious ones. Always seeking to be holy and always sinful, religion will daily be something to be proud of and ashamed of. In fact, an objective acceptance of the reality of religion is a sign of the maturity of the professional's life and dedication.

Love for the values of *faith manifests itself in one's attitudes toward individuals,* not only those who are like-minded to ourselves but also toward those whose views differ from our own. Many contemporary leaders who suffered from former leaders who imposed their own will on their followers will be aware of the need to guard against the arrogance that imposes one's own will as if it were God's.

Contemporary Christians must be people who can collaborate with those with whom they work, whether team members, central leaders, or colleagues at all levels of the organization. *Collaboration is an integral part of spirituality,* since it is the administrative model that best portrays the nature of shared faith. Seen as a form of ongoing discernment, collaboration both requires and teaches virtues that are essential in any spiritual leadership. Collaboration touches the core of a leader's life, since it is not merely a way of doing things more efficiently but a way of being a faith-filled person more authentically.

The Christian is dedicated to proclaiming the truth and needs *always to be open to search for that truth* without ever absolutizing any channel or stage in the quest, but remaining ever open to the newness of God's loving presence and vital revelation. The believer's task is a prophetic one, to be a focus for honesty without counting the pain and persecution that this commitment now brings to anyone who challenges the increasing insecurity of the self-assured.

Spirituality for a spiritual leader *means being a listener to the world*—its political and social events, the signs of the times, people's hopes and joys, anguish and pain. All religious growth takes place in interaction with the world around us, amidst the trends and transitoriness of history. Students of culture, history, and contemporary life, spiritual leaders can make the message of faith relevant to an ever-changing world whose new hopes and new needs can find responses in the reproclaimed word of God.

For contemporary leaders *spirituality is a balance between self-lessness and self-care*—both go together and safeguard each other from unhealthy exaggerations. The spiritual leader's extended availability to lovingly serve the people entrusted to him or her by an organization, by society, and by the Lord must not degenerate into self-neglect that can lead to burnout or simply to a sense of emptiness and purposelessness when the service ends. Each spiritual leader needs to know what is negotiable in the hardships and tensions of service of others. Rather, the generosity and enthusiasm that characterize a spiritual leader's selfless service are nourished by time and distance away from the place and people of one's daily working life. Any vocation or career can soon become a routine job, but nourishing self-care can insure it does not degenerate into approaches spiritual leaders never thought would occur in them.

Along the lines of self-care, spiritual leaders' dedication can grow when *strengthened by deep friendships,* and for those who are married, by a deep relationship with their spouse—both relationships providing levels of intimacy needed for integral growth and a mature development of one's sexuality. Contemporary spirituality of public life needs to be complemented by a spirituality of intimacy. Deep, intimate relationships enrich one's ministry by providing a core experience that not only nourishes, but also models love, community building, concern, and service of a significant other which is the basic attitude of a spiritual leader.

A dedicated believer's spirituality *includes an openness to the future* and a readiness to move on. Like Paul each one can say, "Not that I have already obtained this or have already reached the goal; but I press on to make it my own, because Christ Jesus has made me his own" (Phil 3:12).

Christian spirituality for leaders *includes acceptance of responsibility to correct institutional failures* of the past or present, especially structured injustice such as the negative attitude toward women, unhealthy working environments, unjust salary scales, pollution, and all forms of social irresponsibility. All those dedicated to service are called not only to reaffirm equality but to reclaim what was lost by prior failures. Thus, we not only dedicate ourselves to fight the exclusion of women and capitalize on their commitment, but also to rediscovering the feminine in all of us and channeling it to our integrated spiritual growth and to new enriching models of leadership.

Spirituality for a Christian involved in leadership *includes rejoicing in oneself*—celebrating one's gifts and accepting one's weaknesses. Christian tradition has always valued self-knowledge, and the spiritual leader's realistic view of self clarifies what goals or tasks are possible for the minister and what are unreal expectations. Leaders need to be men and women of peace, joy, and enthusiasm, for they are among the community as models of hope. While bringing these qualities to their service of others through leadership, they will also find that their faithful dedication brings them these very qualities with a new vitality. Spiritual leaders with the courage of their convictions are rare. Theirs is what Bolman and Deal call "an uncommon journey of spirit."

3. Ongoing Development of Spiritual Leadership

For a spiritual leader the motivating values of life are the core values of his or her original "faith." In some way it is true to say that these values are perennial, yet at the same time new circumstances will call forth new responses never seen before but resulting from a new embodiment of the same foundational, core values. *Spiritual leaders reverence perennial values but interpret them in transitory forms.* So, spirituality evolves and does so in varied ways as new generations of leaders find new ways of living out their sense of faith and call. This requires a spirit of openness to new, more relevant ways of living the core values. In fact the exploratory dimension of spirituality preserves its relevance. All interpretations, including the Bible's, are provisional and passing. Christian spiritual leadership must relate these values to present trends and developments.

Spirituality is a response to a fundamental demand in the depths of one's heart that urges us to take life seriously, giving primacy to God-directed values. Thus, there are three essential components of Christian spirituality. First, rootedness—the perennial values must always be the same. Second, interpretation—the essential and unchanging core values need to be lived with the same spirit and life as they always were, which often requires that their articulation will change in order that the essence remain. Third, discovery—an attitude of constant openness to the Spirit's challenge in each generation, calling spiritual leaders and communities to give new life to the rooted and interpreted call.

We live at a time when people are more appreciative of the variety of traditions and spiritualities within Christianity. Many believers have had plenty of ecumenical experiences, shared in spiritual movements, traveled quite a lot, and lived in intercultural communities. They have witnessed the variety of expressions of dedication to faith and appreciate them as signs of the rich gifts dedicated spiritual leaders can share with each other.

While Christian spirituality evidences itself in the personal experiences of believers in their various traditions, it also acknowledges that while the underlying faith should be the same for all Christian life, real *spirituality grows out of actual daily experience of each of us with our own history.* The inspiration of the Holy Spirit faithfully provokes in believers the rebirth of the living teachings of Jesus, but does so in dialogue with the psychological, social, cultural, and local conditions of each individual. In fact, such changes often lead to changes in fundamental consciousness that call forth profound changes in spirituality.

Since spirituality is ever changing and ever new, it requires in religious seekers *a willingness to empty oneself in readiness for the newness of insight and revelation.* Even our latest understandings of God can block our encounter with God, and so we can never turn our own present religious experiences into idols that thwart union with divine life. Christian spirituality leads to integrated development and touches the very depths of a person, calling for a unified development of one's personality. It invests our entire way of thinking and living, transforming the whole of life.

4. Spiritual Leadership and the Future

Many elements that make up the fabric of our spiritual lives will need to be rewoven with stronger threads to withstand contemporary changes and tensions. Spirituality consists in men's and women's grace-filled efforts to become who they are capable of being. Since God is always drawing us to divine life, human efforts are not so much attempts to move forward and grow, but rather they are attempts to cut false values that keep us from God, to thwart our own resistance to God's grace. Each life is a vocation to become more than we already are—personally, socially, cosmically, and wholistically. Sin is the thwarting of this growth potential by refusing to be more than we are now, to be for others in love, to be with others in community. Christian spirituality always implies a willingness to live in insecurity.

Spirituality, then, is letting our life develop in the love-filled atmosphere of God's grace, where we grow naturally and effortlessly, provided we remove all hindrances to growth. Christian spirituality of the future will include perennial values and some new focuses. The great Jesuit theologian, Karl Rahner, suggested five characteristics of the spirituality of the future: 1. The new spirituality will remain the old spirituality of the church, 2. It will concentrate on what is essential to piety, 3. It will live out of a solitary and immediate experience of God, 4. It will emphasize a sense of Christian community, 5. It will embody a new sense of community.[4] Thus our faithful response to the heart of the great tradition of the Lord will lead to a personal experience of divine life, shared in community, and manifested to the world in the church.

I have suggested elsewhere[5] that the common components of a perennial Christian spirituality are a sense of baptismal vocation, an awareness that life is grace and gift of God, a commitment to evangelical life, and an openness to new priorities. These common components are seen in four trends, four major thrusts of contemporary spirituality: ecclesial, incarnational, service-oriented, and liberational. Each generation strives faithfully to respond to the implications of the Sermon on the Mount for changed times. This renewed and renewing response is to God in worship, to Christ in his redeeming love, to oneself in openness to destiny, to others in their mutual growth, and to the world in its history. This is the spirituality of the future that will be embodied in the lives of dedicated spiritual leaders, and will include among other things the following components.

"The Christian of the future will be a mystic or he or she will not exist at all....by mysticism we mean...a genuine experience of God emerging from the very heart of our existence."[6] A person of interiority and faith, the Christian spiritual leader's experience will flow from personal experiences of God's mercy, forgiveness, compassion, and love. Thus, he or she does not share the life of a particular religion with others but the fruit of his or her own life with God. This experience of faith leads one to live with a sense of wonder, appreciating that the whole of life is aflame with the presence of God. However, life in the Spirit is nurtured in solitude, where we reaffirm faith and reexperience what we believe in. This faith is the source of the radical dedication of hope that sustains the spiritual leader, motivating him or her in the work of transformation. This hope is a hope that produces enthusiasm, zeal, and disinterested sharing of a mystical encounter with God. The believer's experience of God produces the life of faith and hope that results from and causes love. After all, mysticism means not knowing, but experiencing that God is love. It gives rise to a passionate love for life, beauty, and wisdom, a thirsting for life itself—a power that drives us to union. This love is an integration of eros, philia, and agape; the passionate love of mind and body, friendship love, and the faith and hope-filled love of Christian community. Thus, spirituality, the mystical experience of the living God, is the level of our faith, hope, and love that as Christians we live and foster in others. "This potential to become a mystic, an ordinary mystic, is the most important calling of our life. It is growth in the gradual awareness of experiencing and personally communicating with a loving God; it is a particular person's living faith experienced and integrated into an ordinary but deep, daily way of life."[7]

Mystical union leads in the spiritual leader to an urgent longing to participate in the redeeming love of Christ. Having experienced God's love, having grasped that God is love, having deepened one's capacity for love, the believer finds that love demands action, conquers fear, unites the separated, empowers the weak, transcends human smallness, and conspires to spread itself—what Matthew Fox calls "a marriage of mysticism and social justice."[8]

At the core of each person there is a zone that is naturally divine, and there we find freedom and love, mutually authenticating each other. Those Christians who are open to the action of the Holy Spirit at this level of life yearn to give birth in others to freedom and love. Thus, compassion with self, others, religion, and the world becomes a natural response and pursues justice as a contemporary goal of true wisdom. Perhaps more than anything else, the redeeming love of Christ is the triumph of nonviolence over all who would crucify whatever diminishes their selfish interests. This prophetic stance may well cause more crucifixion in the decades ahead, but it is the only authentic embodiment of the Christian's experience of the living God and the redeeming love of Christ.

Christian spirituality is also a faith- and love-filled response in hope to one's destiny under God. The personal sense of mission—not a transitory task to accomplish but a destiny in the plan of God—is discoverable in the true solitude of one who is aware of need, receptive, and open to grace. Such a solitude is not selfish; rather "it is indispensable for the development of a capacity for self-giving. Those who do not experience solitude before God do not really possess themselves; hence they cannot truly give themselves away."[9] It is in prayerful solitude that Christian quality of life begins. This "awakening of self to the Spirit"[10] is an experience of vocation in which "the lonely responsibility of the individual in his or her decision of faith is necessary and required in a way much more radical than it was in former times."[11] The leader's response requires perseverance and courage, a rededication to total dependence on God, and a new discovery of simplicity of life, a daily commitment to be on a pilgrimage that is filled with hope in God's promises, and a sense of peaceful acceptance of oneself—one's body and its rhythms, one's mind and heart with their energies, one's spirit with its peaceful dissatisfaction.

Christian spirituality is a participation in faith and in the life of God, and the divine life is friendship. So the finest dimensions of friendship should also be part of the believer's life and message. In friendship and solidarity, Christians discover a deeper understanding of the message they proclaim, are enriched with an awareness of common vision and shared purpose, and are reenergized through mutuality, coresponsibility, and the unity of faith. Life with others will have its inner tension and conflict and its outreach struggles for human rights wherever violated or threatened. However, this life consists especially in mutual support in the work of community building, in bearing the burdens of service of others, in enduring the inadequacies of organizations, in countering the legalism and neglect of many contemporary organizations.

Spirituality is lived out in interaction with the world, seen statically in some aspects of the environment and dynamically in political processes. Early Christians went off to the desert to show their dedication to Christ, but today's desert is the contemporary world and society with their large-scale abuse of God's gifts. Each

Christian will develop a sociocritical approach to the world, living as a professional irritant to its many distortions. Joyfully and gratefully receiving creation, the believer will model a life of simplicity and authentic enjoyment in a nonconsumeristic challenge to false values. Matthew Fox strongly proclaims, "Chronos—the ultimate consumer and the ultimate waster—is the god of Western civilization, encouraging us in our consumption and waste of youth, of Mother Earth, of minorities, of imagination itself, of mysticism, of our powers of compassion, of our sexual energy, of good work. We consume and waste our prophets and our mystics. We are wasting Christ and Christianity as well."[12] Thus, Christians will need to live as the conscience of society. People of hope, spiritual leaders should be noted for their creativity, their ongoing participation in world history, seeing this personal and communal sharing in the divine life as an optimistic blessing of the world by those who truly love it.

Toward every aspect of life, spirituality of the future for the spiritual leader will bring a critical attitude of constant challenge, evaluation, and redirection, a hopeful courage that struggles will bear fruit, an openness to learn, to be enriched, to be corrected, and to be challenged, a trusting submission to the wonderful God, an attitude of magnificence in all that one does,[13] a dedication to solidarity with people from all walks of life, and a life immersed in peaceful joy. In this way spiritual leaders enrich themselves and the people and world they love and serve.

CONCLUSION: THE SPIRITUAL EXPERIENCE OF LEADING OTHERS— AN INVITATION

1. Introduction

So much has been written on leadership in the last decade or so, and yet there is so much experience of failed leadership. The scientific requirement to quantitatively document this quality or that has added much to our knowledge of leadership theory. Yet many individuals who supposedly embody these theories have often ended up as failures, and many of the model organizations studied over and over again have ended up as unjust oppressors of their own stakeholders. One of the constant emphases of this book is that it is not possible to separate leadership from life; rather it is part of an integrated approach to the whole of life. Unfortunately many in potential leadership positions are known for failed relationships, frequent broken marriages, and for being strangers to their own spouse and children. Such individuals should not be hailed as leaders. Others who have frequented the talk shows as experts on leadership have ended up as abusers of society, preying on their businesses to the detriment of workers and society in general. Clearly these are not leaders. It has become a disheartening practice to look back over the recent shameful endings to so-called leaders' careers. Frustration replaces the hope we placed in gifted individuals. They became arrogant, failed to facilitate growth of others as they could have, ended as blind visionaries and do-nothing managers. Potential leaders in

121

whom we placed our hope became entrenched in their narcissism, void of genuine concern for others, victims of leader pathology. Empirical approaches to leadership will always need to be pursued, but with an awareness of their transitory nature. We need more and more courageous leaders who will dedicate themselves to a new style of living that will change their leadership too. That we have few empirical studies on spiritual leadership does not mean we cannot evaluate spiritual values; seminaries, ministry training programs, pastoral counseling programs have been doing this successfully for years. For too long we have studied leadership as if it were a separate category of life, whereas it is simply a quality of life that affects everything one does and can thus be applied to the context of leadership.

Leadership studies evidence a growing movement toward integrated and holistic approaches to leadership that emphasizes one's inner self, spirit, and soul, and they focus on maturity, credibility, wisdom, and love. Contemporary studies stress the person of the leader and his or her sense of call to serve others and pursue a common vision that affects not just the working environment but personal, family, institutional, and societal environments in an ever-expanding influence of the dedicated leader. Leadership for those who are called to serve others is never static but always dynamic, growing and maturing through stages that enrich one's life as well as one's leadership.

Spiritual leadership is a model of leadership that unites what we do and how we do it with who we are and what values motivate us in life. It is a form of principle-centered leadership that proposes approaches to others and to organizations that are self-transcending. It draws together personal talents, community-building skills, managerial competence, and organizational renewal within the context of response to the challenges of the Spirit. Great leaders are grounded in motivating values such as inner integrity, shared vision, inspiration, pursuit of mission, an awareness of human interdependence, constant humility, service of others, courage, and an enthusiastic challenge of others to be their best.

Spiritual leadership, which an increasing number of authors consider the only viable form of leadership for the future, is not just another management style; rather it is the result of a change of life, a conversion, a breakthrough to a new vision of one's role in the world. It is the result of a deliberate personal choice that is motivated by love. This book invites readers to reflect on how they see themselves as leaders and whether this model or something like it can be the motivation for their lives too.

Spiritual leadership essentially means focusing on others rather than oneself. It is a move from self-centeredness to other-centeredness and even self-transcendence. This has very practical conclusions that impact the leader's life. It means leading others to lead themselves and then being ready to step aside as others come forward to lead. You lead others to lead themselves by influencing others to be visionaries, gradually making them aware of their own gifts and their need to utilize the gifts for the wider community. Influencing others in such a way that they will eventually lead begins by getting them used to change and crisis, working with them from the start to realize that they have a contribution to the shared vision, training and coaching them to become visionaries, collaborating with them, and respectfully accepting their contributions so that they truly feel they are partners in a common cause.

Throughout the leadership of a spiritual leader the effectiveness of leadership is dependent on the leader's integrity. This contemporary constitutive component of leadership reminds us yet again of the congruence there must be between one's words and actions, one's vision and strategic planning, one's fundamental values and management priorities, one's inner way of thinking and one's outward professional life. Integrity is particularly strengthened by the leader's constant care to build a trusting environment.

This book is presented as a series of reflections. A spiritual leader needs wisdom that comes from inner calm and peace. It is from this reflective approach to leadership that integration emerges. The spiritual leader takes care to develop stillness, inspiration, concentration, and silence that give rise to the ability to see things in the big picture, see everyone's role in community, see the shared vision that an institution holds, and see an institution's role in society. The leader must see what others do not see, and this is impossible without reflection.

Reflection enables a leader to see the links between individual and institutional life and to appreciate that there can be no genuine leadership without the transformation of organizational life. So, a leader promotes organizational well-being, empowers individuals and teams, and restructures an organization in order to be faithful to its core motivating values. Above all, the spiritual leader knows that organizations grow through their own stages of maturity—growth that must be managed and even facilitated.

The various chapters of this book are varied aspects of spiritual leadership that presume that an individual leader's motivation for everything he or she does in life—whether at work, in family, in organizations, or in society as a whole—comes from a series of values that form the basis of the leader's faith. Leadership is who one is becoming as one journeys inward to discover the call and destiny of life. This spirituality is never static but always dynamic; fundamental values are ever growing, enriching one's leadership and one's life.

2. An Invitation to Lead

The English-speaking world tends to use the term *leadership* too freely. We speak about political leaders, religious leaders, leaders of industry, military leaders, and so on. But most of these people are not leaders at all; they are, at the most, good managers. In many cases people presume those in higher positions are leaders, and they even presume it themselves, but they do not do what leaders do; they do what managers do. Using the term *leadership* when we are not really talking about leadership confuses the issues and sometimes leads some managers to think they are leaders. Terms such as "transactional leadership," which should be "transactional management," or "managerial leadership" as if there were such a thing as leadership without managerial skills, cloud the debate. Moreover, a person can be charismatic and have influence on others but never become a leader.

While many managers will never become leaders, leaders do need to be good managers. According to J. P. Kotter's well-known distinction between management and leadership, management deals with planning, budgeting, organizing, staffing, controlling, and problem solving; whereas leadership deals with establishing direction, aligning people, motivating, and inspiring them.[1] While the latter includes much of the former, the reverse is not the case. Many managers have remained so all their lives either because they know no better or because their organization never challenged them to anything else. Kotter suggested that some practices within an organization inhibit the emergence of leadership: lots of short-term technical jobs that do not require much thought or strategy, vertical career moves, rapid promotions, reward system based on short-term results. He then suggested that others promote the emergence of leadership: challenging assignments early in a career, extreme examples in role models—either good or bad—where the lessons are clear, assignments that broaden one's knowledge, relationships, and motivation.[2] He also suggests that an organization can create leadership capacity in managers through sophisticated recruiting efforts, an attractive working environment, challenging opportunities, identification of worker potential and needs, and planning.[3] While these are excellent suggestions, they do not automatically produce leadership. Management is a task, a job to be accomplished while one is in a certain environment. It is a position in a structure. Leadership is a vocation, a faithful living of core values that motivate life. Leadership is always part of who you are and is not limited to a given environment. It refers to who you are for yourself, for your family, and for others. It is a sense of destiny in the world.

Marcic may well be close to the issue of what constitutes leadership when she reminds her readers that there are five dimensions of life that must come together before major organizational change and the emergence of genuine leadership; there must be change on five levels: physical, intellectual, emotional, volitional, and spiritual.[4] She is right in indicating that authentic leadership touches every part of one's personality. Leadership is a call that affects every facet of one's personality. However, it is a call and to put it bluntly no one calls himself or herself. It could be that followers call an individual to lead. It could be that some particular circumstance or event calls forth an individual to respond by leading others. It could be a crisis that calls an individual to lead others through it and out of it. It could be a sense of personal destiny. Of course, it could also be an awareness of call embedded in a religious tradition or in a personal encounter with God in prayer.

I have referred to all of these as a faith experience that leads one to live differently. Of utmost importance is to be aware that call—from whatever source one thinks it comes—must be verified and authenticated by others. Furthermore, call is not permanent or universal; it may be for some followers but not for other people, it may be for a certain event but not others, it may be for a limited period but it passes, it could be for some member of a family but it is not thereby inherited by other family members, it has little to do with position although position can be an opportunity. If leadership is a call, then no one calls himself or herself to be a leader. A person could offer self, or those senior in a hierarchy might present someone as a leader, but it is followers alone who verify that this person is a leader and reward his or her service with a genuine call.

However, while leadership is a call, and no one calls himself or herself, plenty of people are called but they are not ready when the call comes. It is important to realize that one can prepare oneself for the call. We have seen so many concrete practices that individuals can implement to foster a sense of service of others, or to live with integrity, or to work toward a shared vision, or to become a reflective person, or to give priority to spiritual and integrative values. All these can be preparations for those who look forward to leading should the occasion arise or for those who are already in a potential leadership position but are not recognized as leaders by their followers.

Some writers refer to this change in direction from management to leadership, or from potential leadership to actualized leadership, as a breakthrough experience, a transformation, a liberation, or a search for excellence. Whether this experience is individual or organizational, I have consistently referred to this change as a conversion. The first words uttered by Jesus in the Gospels call for a conversion, a word which means a change of heart. However, in Jesus' culture and times the heart was not the source of love and affection but the source of knowledge and vision. Therefore, the first statement of Jesus to those who wish to mature as human beings is "get a new outlook on life," "get a new vision," "get a new set of priorities." Michael Carey, who sees the call to leadership as a conversion, refers to this decision to live by a new outlook, new vision, and a new set of priorities as a "fundamental option," that one great decision in life that motivates everything else that we do. The resulting leader is competent, motivates followers to end values such as justice, service, community, and love, contributes to social change, and satisfies the authentic needs of self and followers.[5]

Many who would like to be leaders or who are in potential leadership positions, seek to professionally improve themselves in study, workshops, courses, and degree programs, hoping to find the skills, the behaviors, the experiences that might enable them to be the leaders they yearn to be. They are all good but inadequate. Rather they should go deep within themselves to find the authentic self, purpose in life, and personal destiny. Then they should begin to live by the values that are part of their new outlook on life, embody the vision and values of spiritual leadership no matter the cost, focus on influencing others to be leaders, seek always to be a person of integrity, let no day pass without time in reflection, contribute in whatever possible ways to organizational well-being, and see self as a spiritual leader. These of course were the chapters of this book and some of the values to be pursued.

3. Effective Leadership

In this book we have spoken of aspects of spiritual leadership. Of course we must eventually see evidence that this form of leadership is more effective than others; otherwise we might as well revert to the example of the first-rate autocrats or benevolent autocrats of whom we all have experience. However, effectiveness itself will need to be judged differently including what happens to the leader, follower, and society in the long run as a result of a change in leadership style. It may well be true that effective leaders within the organization may go unrecognized by the higher-ups in the structure, but their effectiveness remains. Furthermore, when judging effectiveness in leadership, we must be sensitive to gender-specific assumptions. Finally, we need to be aware that effectiveness varies dependent on availability of resources, quality of workforce, impact of shared vision, and even people's moods.

Spiritual leaders of the kind we have described are effective, followers attribute legitimate leadership to them, and in turn they model their own behavior on the self-sacrificing behavior of the spiritual leader.[6] These leaders have a passion for a shared vision, they inspire confidence in others, and generate excitement and enthusiasm. They are not leaders by default because of their position in a structure; they are leaders by vocation. Power is not as important to them as leadership.[7] These people give the impression that they are on the right track and moving in the right direction. They are people of commitment and integrity; flexible provided there remains a common dedication to excellence and common vision.

These leaders take good care of themselves, maintain an exciting life, have deep and lasting relationships, keep focused on life of which the job is just a part. In other words, they are people of perspective. Yes! they can make tough decisions, and live by hard-hitting principles, but they know how important or unimportant those hard issues really are. They know they have a uniqueness to contribute to the leadership roles they have, and they preserve this uniqueness from the deterioration that comes with excessive stress, tension, and egoism.

The spiritual leader has broad interests that go beyond the immediate task. Bernard Bass insisted on the importance of such breadth of vision. "Superior leadership performance—transformational leadership—occurs when leaders broaden and elevate the interests of their employees, when they generate awareness and acceptance of the purposes and mission of the group, and when they stir their employees to look beyond their own self-interest for the good of the group."[8] In implementing the task the spiritual leader maintains commitment, constant challenge of all involved, and continuing connection with coworkers. These qualities "when combined...form a strong bridge to high performance in the new workplace."[9] This kind of leader is proactive and begins his or her dedication to effective leadership by creating a workplace environment that leads to greater creativity, effectiveness, and mutual empowerment,[10] and follows this with effective listening and careful response to the input of others. He or she will maintain this effective feedback throughout the relationship with followers.[11] This leader's attitudes of service to the individual and to the organization enable him or her to enlist the cooperation of others, to coach and mentor them during the progress, and to monitor the results. Moreover, the leader is able to do this in a nonthreatening way since he or she has taken care to build good relationships with individuals and a deeper sense of community. We have seen that this spiritual leader by allowing others to learn from failure facilitates a positive approach to risk-taking and crisis management. This naturally allows this kind of leader to effectively delegate authority to others who know they are trusted, will be supported throughout the task, will be helped in times of difficulty and failure to refocus, and will be appreciated for their dedication.[12]

More than anything else effective leadership refers to motivating others to attain common goals. People have employment because they need a livelihood; but people work even without employment, or work differently when employed because they are motivated. One of the key qualities of a spiritual leader that motivates others is discretionary commitment—that dedication over and above the professional commitment necessary to do a good job. This is one of the most contagious aspects of the leader's dedication. The leader seeks input in the setting of goals, generates ownership of the goals, determines worker input into strategies, and mobilizes effort and perseverance in attaining the goals.[13] The leader will not forget to evaluate, refocus, and celebrate success in goal achievement.

Effective leadership today requires continuing education and an ongoing willingness to relearn how to learn; the leader is always a learner reflecting on the past, grasping the values of the present, and looking to the future. These leaders make their community into a learning community. Barrett comments: "Appreciative learning cultures accentuate the successes of the past, evoke images of possible futures, and create a spirit of restless, ongoing enquiry that empowers members to new levels of activity."[14] Barrett goes on to point out that these appreciative learning cultures give rise to new competencies: affirmative, expansive, generative, and collaborative.

Effective leadership needs heart not drive; its focus is caring for people and doing together what you are capable of. The spiritual leader feels the urge to discover and draw out qualities that lie in everyone. Now and again a leader should ask himself or herself: why do you think that people need you? Why do you need to do this particular job? What is the best experience you have had as a leader and why do you think it was good? How have you dealt with the "weakest member" of the group? In what situations have your best qualities come forth? What do followers like best in you? If you were no longer a part of this group would you be missed and if so why? Effective leadership is a matter of faith in self and in others, of hope in the value of the common shared mission and in its impact on others, and of love made visible in all we do.

4. A Model of Spiritual Leadership

A model is a tool that helps to explain the stages of development that produce spiritual leadership. Every model is a sign that gives us insight into the reality of leadership, and every model is also a symbol, but it also evokes the kind of response it seeks to encourage in others. But models are more than signs and symbols in so far as we use them to critically explain the reality in question. Following a period of disillusionment we have seen some excellent insights into the use of models in leadership development.[15] We have also seen some proposals that are overwhelming in their details and therefore not usable. I seek to avoid the mind-boggling diagrams encountered in many journal articles of recent years. James Hunt commented on a similar experience, saying that some writers are "beguiled by the esoteric statistical packages available."[16] The proposal that follows is integrative, that is, it avoids the dualism between who one is and what one does, and it is holistic, that is, it includes every aspect of life. I propose the following model in seven steps.

1. Remote preparation
2. Conversion—a new way of looking at things
   conversion to the self one can become
   conversion to the community one can be a part of
3. Acceptance of call
4. Implementation of the vision in action
5. Utilization of a mentor or guide
   or facilitation of peer support in mutual mentoring
6. Evaluation
   self-evaluation
   professional evaluation by others
7. Reflection on one's leadership

1. Remote preparation for spiritual leadership includes study, discussion with others, and reflection. The new way of looking at things that really begins the journey to spiritual leadership needs to be based on different ideas than one currently has. This preparation requires inner peace and energy; it balances time alone and time with others, searching for the new vision that stretches one out to possess a different perspective on life. This preparation time helps one discover one's deepest personal needs, hopes, and dreams, as well as the deepest needs and hopes of others that one may seek or be called to serve. If a person has good material on which to reflect and dedicated people with whom to share, then there is a chance of thinking about leadership in a totally different way as well as finding a new meaning in life, a new sense of personal destiny.

2. Conversion is a new outlook on life and a new set of priorities. People of faith will consider it a gift, but it is also something we consciously or unconsciously prepare for through our open-mindedness and open-heartedness to our study, discussion, and reflection. It is a moral and value movement that provokes a new way of thinking of self and of thinking about community. On a personal and individual level conversion calls one to accept one's own greatness, one's own importance for others, one's own uniqueness. This is authentic humility. It means having perspectives on life that are loaded with values and having standards for their own sake.

Conversion means living motivated by love; it is the beginning of the journey from self-centeredness to other-centeredness.

Conversion is incomplete if it produces a lonely charismatic who thinks he or she is a gift to everyone else. Rather, authentic conversion always includes a deeper awareness of community. Conversion is a new presence to oneself for sure, but also to others in community. As part of a new outlook on life, conversion to community enables us to appreciate the gifts of everyone, our own incompleteness without others, and the profound value of shared vision and goals. When Joe Batten calls us to be all we can be in community he stresses that the key ingredients are "caring, sharing, and forgiving."[17] Conversion to community is a very practical change in life that includes the sensitivity to others of which Batten speaks, but also the acknowledgment of the reality of politics in groups. A leader will always need to know his or her own boundaries in politics—what you are willing and unwilling to do as part of the political process. This can also remind the leader that while dedicated to community, a great leader also stands slightly apart from the community to preserve his or her own independence in leading. This must be a healthy distancing that does not end in "righteous separatism" or "arrogant self-interest" that can lead to the destruction of community.[18] Conversion must eventually prove itself in changed lives individually and in community. Over time it is a chance for our practice to catch up with where our heart claims to be.

3. Acceptance of call comes when one understands the basic values that motivate life and knows that one has these values in trust for others. It is the deliberate commitment to live in a new way with new priorities and to make all judgments in light of these values. In so far as it is an awareness that one has something to say and do for the benefit of others, this leadership is a form of prophecy. "Prophecy" is a Greek word which means "to speak on behalf of." It does not need to imply the future, but rather refers to words of love, compassion, and meaning that one can speak to others on behalf of God or transcendent values. The call can come from a variety of sources, but the leader-to-be must have the insight to recognize the moment of call, whether it is explicit, a job description, an invitation by others, or embedded

in a faith experience. This acceptance of call results from the awareness of role and destiny in this world. It implies accepting one's own stature and importance to others and the humble realization that one has an important place in society.

4. Implementing the vision in action is the only way to show integrity and to gain credibility. A leader cannot accept a call in words alone but only through the implementing of the vision in daily decisions, actions, judgments, budgeting, and planning. Since the vision is both individual and communitarian, so too the implementing will be both individual and through common group vision and shared values. So, the leader we envision will also work though networks and teams, seeking to implement the vision with others. This is the time when the leader utilizes management skills and the skills of the spiritual leader.

5. "Utilize a mentor or guide" is an excellent recommendation for today's leaders. It preserves a leader from arrogance and maintains the focus on the contributions of others. It facilitates discernment when the leader needs to make key decisions. It preserves an important role for shared wisdom, prudent guidance, and constant refocusing of direction. Sometimes a leader cannot find the gifted mentor he or she would like to find, and then needs to get together with other similarly deprived leaders to help each other through mutual mentoring. This is not the desirable way to handle mentoring but it is better than nothing.

6. Evaluation is a necessity for every prudent leader who feels called to spiritual leadership. Seeing one's role in the bigger picture and checking up on one's faithfulness to the vision and one's effectiveness in implementing it keep a leader well-focused. This evaluation on fidelity to call and realistic and effective implementing of it can be done by oneself, and should be done frequently. It should also be the responsibility of others—workers, peers, and supervisors. Whether done by oneself or by others, this evaluation is basically a reflection on what has been done in light of the way one wanted to do things. It means thinking back to the times of enthusiastic dedication to the vision of spiritual leadership to ask if one still measures up to the commitment made. Some people refer to those past times of clearly focused dedication as "dangerous memories," dangerous because they

were the times that called for change and transformation. Now we ask if we were faithful. This evaluation will be ongoing and may well be just a few minutes each day asking ourselves how we can improve what we are doing. Professional evaluations by others at various levels in an organization are very useful, provided they are clearly focused on the original goals and vision. Reporting of the evaluation must be honest and specific.

7. Reflection on one's leadership is perhaps the most significant assurance for success. This personal reflection can lead to new insights on leadership and be the transition to a new cycle of conversion; reflection ends the cycle and is at the same time the remote preparation for a new phase of growth in leadership development.

5. Conclusion

In this conclusion and throughout the book I have criticized aspects of contemporary leadership. This does not mean I think I can do any better, but rather that I feel very strongly that the direction of many, if not most, who struggle to implement leadership in their lives is wrong. Good-hearted individuals who wish to serve as leaders need to ask themselves whether they are satisfied with the fruits of their efforts. If not, then they should conclude that the model of leadership they are using is not working. Such individuals need to rethink the meaning of leadership in their lives. Burt Nanus, in a section on vision as key to leadership, quotes a Chinese proverb that points out that unless you change direction you are likely to arrive where you are headed.[19] The major theme of this book is that we need to look at leadership as an integral aspect of our entire lives; spiritual leadership that brings transformation to our personal, family, social, and societal parts of life. We need to change direction. I have stressed that spirituality is always growing, never static; it is the daily yearning for the "more" that we can achieve. Ritscher says, "spirituality is an experience of depth in life; it is living with heart rather than superficiality."[20] The original "faith" experience that gives birth to one's spiritual leadership provides a reference point to look back to, while also providing a deep peace that permeates one's efforts, a daily challenge to become who we saw ourselves called to be, and the resilience to rise and try again when our efforts are inadequate. Each of us is called to become the best leader we are capable of being. We do not imitate anyone else, but see their gifts and internalize their values; then we ourselves become leaders—each one a unique leader.

NOTES

1. Introduction

1. See Robert K. Greenleaf, *Servant Leadership: A Journey into the Nature of Legitimate Power and Greatness* (New York/Mahwah, NJ: Paulist Press, 1977), 7.

2. See Lee G. Bolman and Terrence E. Deal, *Leading with Soul: An Uncommon Journey of Spirit* (San Francisco: Jossey-Bass, 1995), 15–25.

3. Mary L. Pulley, *Losing Your Job—Reclaiming Your Spirit* (San Francisco: Jossey-Bass, 1997); see chapter six, "Dark Times," and chapter seven, "Soul Searching."

4. But why say "spiritual values," or "spiritual leadership," as if there was some inadequacy with material leadership? Older literature made a distinction between spiritual and material levels of life, considering the former good and the latter weak. Nowadays, we tend to still use this vocabulary, as in "spiritual leadership," but use it in a more integrative way. "Spiritual" now means permeating the whole of life with the very best values that motivate a person.

5. Robert K. Greenleaf, *The Power of Servant Leadership*, ed. Larry C. Spears (San Francisco: Berrett-Koehler, 1998), 93. See also throughout this work where he gives the components of a life deferred: a lifestyle of greatness, cultivation of one's own creativeness, building a new morality, growth in wisdom, trust, sense of realism, learning to live with anxiety.

Chapter 1

1. Jeanne M. Wilson, Jill George, Richard S. Wellins, and William C. Byham, *Leadership Trapeze* (San Francisco: Jossey-Bass, 1994), 67.

2. See John P. Kotter, *What Leaders Really Do* (Boston: Harvard Business School Press, 1999), 62: "Despite leadership's growing importance, the on-the-job experiences of most people undermine their ability to lead."

3. W. G. Bennis, "Transformative Power and Leadership," in *Leadership and Organizational Culture*, ed. T. J. Sergiovanni and J. E. Corbally, 259–60 (Urbana: University of Illinois Press, 1984).

4. Alan Bryman, *Leadership and Organizations* (London: Routledge and Kegan Paul, 1986), 198.

5. See Daniel Sankowsky, "The Charismatic Leader as Narcissist: Understanding the Abuse of Power," *Organizational Dynamics* 23 (Spring 1995): 61.

6. Gregory P. Smith, *The New Leader: Bringing Creativity and Innovation to the Workplace* (Delray Beach, FL: St. Lucie Press, 1997), 19.

7. Michel Syrett and Clare Hogg, eds., "Take Me to Your Leader," in *Frontiers of Leadership: An Essential Reader* (Oxford: Blackwell Publishers, 1992), 13, quoting Abraham Zaleznik, *The Managerial Mystique*.

8. See Dorothy Marcic, *Managing with the Wisdom of Love* (San Francisco: Jossey-Bass, 1995), 27.

9. See Warren Black, *The 9 Natural Laws of Leadership* (New York: AMACOM, 1995), 42.

10. See Peter Senge, *The Fifth Discipline: The Art and Practice of the Learning Organization* (New York: Doubleday, 1990), 17–26.

11. Peter Koestenbaum, *Leadership: The Inner Side of Greatness* (San Francisco: Jossey-Bass, 1991), 22.

12. Dennis T. Jaffe, Cynthia D. Scott, and Glenn R. Tobe, *Rekindling Commitment* (San Francisco: Jossey-Bass 1994), xii.

13. The professor was J. B. Ritchie of Brigham Young University, and the episode is referred to in Marcic, *Managing with the Wisdom of Love*, 14.

14. Jaffe and others, *Rekindling Commitment*, 23.

15. Syrett and Hogg, "Take Me to Your Leader," 150.

16. Sankowsky, "The Charismatic Leader as Narcissist," 65.

17. Marcic, *Managing with the Wisdom of Love*, 27.

18. See Kennon L. Callahan, *Effective Church Leadership* (San Francisco: Harper and Row, 1990), 12.

19. See Donna J. Markham, *Spiritlinking Leadership* (New York/Mahwah, NJ: Paulist Press, 1999), 8.

20. Jim Collins, "And the Walls Came Tumbling Down," in *Leading beyond the Walls*, ed. Frances Hesselbein, Marshall Goldsmith, and Ian Somerville (San Francisco: Jossey-Bass, 1999), 25.

21. Keith Grint, *The Arts of Leadership* (Oxford: University Press, 2000), 420.

22. Parker J. Palmer, Foreword, in *Seeker and Servant: The Private Writings of Robert K. Greenleaf*, ed. Anne T. Fraker and Larry C. Spears (San Francisco: Jossey-Bass, 1996), xi.

23. Grint, *The Arts of Leadership*, 419.

24. See Peter Senge, "Leadership in Living Organizations," in *Leading beyond the Walls,* ed. F. Hesselbein and others, 77.

25. Grint, *The Arts of Leadership,* 420.

26. See Koestenbaum, *Leadership;* Mary L. Pulley, *Losing Your Job—Reclaiming Your Spirit* (San Francisco: Jossey-Bass, 1997); Marcic, *Managing with the Wisdom of Love;* Jaffe, Scott, and Tobe, *Rekindling Commitment;* Rushworth M. Kidder, *Shared Values for a Troubled World* (San Francisco: Jossey-Bass, 1994); Lee G. Bolman and Terrence E. Deal, *Leading with Soul: An Uncommon Journey of Spirit* (San Francisco: Jossey-Bass, 1995); Kevin Cashman, *Leadership from the Inside Out* (Provo, UT: Executive Excellence Publishing, 1998); Barbara Maskoff and Gary Wenet, *The Inner Work of Leaders: Leadership as a Habit of Mind* (New York: AMACOM, 2000); Robert J. Spitzer, *The Spirit of Leadership* (Provo, UT: Executive Excellence Publishing, 2000); Russ Moxley, *Leadership and Spirit* (San Francisco: Jossey-Bass, 2000).

27. Bolman and Deal, *Leading with Soul,* 6.

28. Jaffe and others, *Rekindling Commitment,* xii; Jack Hawley, *Reawakening the Spirit in Work* (San Francisco: Berrett-Koehler Publishers, 1993), 1; Bolman and Deal, *Leading with Soul,* 6.

29. Bolman and Deal, *Leading with Soul,* 12.

30. Koestenbaum, *Leadership,* 2.

Chapter 2

1. Richard Hallstein, *Memoirs of a Recovering Autocrat* (San Francisco: Barrett-Koehler, 1992), 36.

2. See Jill W. Graham, "Servant-Leadership in Organizations: Inspirational and Moral," *Leadership Quarterly* 2 (1991): 113.

3. Marcic, *Managing with the Wisdom of Love,* 79, writes: "How are these men (and they were all men) going to create a company based on service when they don't know how to do it themselves? They have wives at home to do everything for them. Basically they just show up and pay the bills. At the office, their secretaries function as office wives, running errands, buying gifts, even making their investments for them. How can I help them to understand what service is all about?"

4. J. M. Kouzes and B. Z. Posner, *The Leadership Challenge: How to Get Extraordinary Things Done in Organizations* (San Francisco: Jossey-Bass, 1988), 184–89, give ten important lessons about learning to lead.

5. See Larry Spears of the Robert K. Greenleaf Center for Servant Leadership, at greenleaf.org, where he identifies the ten critical characteristics of a servant leader as seen in the writings of Robert K. Greenleaf.

The same ten points are available in Greenleaf, *The Power of Servant Leadership*, ed. Larry C. Spears (San Francisco: Berrett-Koehler, 1998), 5–8, and in *The Servant Leader Within* (New York/Mahwah, NJ: Paulist Press, 2003), 16–19.

6. Mary Kate Morse, *The Relationship of Wisdom to Transformational Leadership* (Spokane, WA: Gonzaga University Doctoral Dissertation, 1996), 262, and 242–43.

7. Fred A. Manske, *The Secrets of Effective Leadership* (Germantown, TN: Leadership Education and Development, 1987), 24.

8. Noel M. Tichy and Mary Anne Devanna, *The Transformational Leader* (New York: Wiley, 1986), 134.

9. See Bernard Bass, "From Transactional to Transformational Leadership: Learning to Share the Vision," *Organizational Dynamics* 18 (Winter, 1990): 19–36.

10. James MacGregor Burns, *Leadership* (New York: Harper and Row, 1978), 20.

11. Alan Bryman, *Charisma and Leadership in Organizations* (London: Sage Publications, 1992), 96.

12. Michael Carey, "Transformative Christian Leadership," *Human Development* 12 (1991): 32. Carey is the author who in my judgment has best expressed the distinctions between the positive and negative dimensions of transformational leadership. See also Smith. *The New Leader,* 83, which gives "The Leadership Beatitudes": Be bold and challenge the status quo, Be a risk taker, Be authentic and approachable, Be a role model, Be out and about, Be courageous, and Be inspirational. See also Gilbert W. Fairholm, *The Techniques of Inner Leadership* (Westport, CT: Praeger, 2003), where he develops twenty-one techniques for inner leadership in practice.

13. Bryman, *Charisma and Leadership,* 111.

14. *On Leadership* (New York: The Free Press, 1990), 48–54. See also the tentative list of leadership qualities in Thomas E. Cronin, "Thinking and Learning about Leadership," in *Contemporary Issues in Leadership*, ed. William E. Rosenbach and Robert L. Taylor (San Francisco: Westview Press, 1993), 45–64; those listed in Charles J. Cox and Cary L. Cooper, "Characteristics of the Successful Chief Executive," in *Frontiers of Leadership: An Essential Reader,* ed. Syrett and Hogg, 79–82; and the foundational qualities listed in Ralph M. Stogdill, *Handbook of Leadership* (New York: The Free Press, 1974), 62–63. More detailed explanations of the requirements of leadership can be found in F. Hesselbein and others, *Leading beyond the Walls,* part III.

15. J. W. McLean and William Weitzel, *Leadership: Magic, Myth, or Method* (New York: AMACOM, 1992), 203.

16. Pulley, *Losing Your Job—Reclaiming Your Spirit*, 221.

17. See J. M. Kouzes and B. Z. Posner, *Credibility: How Leaders Gain and Lose It, Why People Demand It* (San Francisco: Jossey-Bass, 1993), 235.

18. James A. Ritscher, "Spiritual Leadership," in *Transforming Leadership: From Vision to Results*, ed. John D. Adams (Alexandria, VA: Miles River Press, 1986), 69.

19. See Cronin, "Thinking and Learning about Leadership," 59.

20. See Warren G. Bennis and B. Nanus, *Leaders: The Strategies for Taking Charge* (New York: Harper and Row, 1985).

21. See Jay A. Conger and Rabinda N. Kanugo, *Charismatic Leadership: The Elusive Factor in Organizational Effectiveness* (San Francisco: Jossey-Bass, 1988), 324–35.

22. See Kouzes and Posner, *The Leadership Challenge*, 49–53. The authors suggest the following: 1. Treat every job as an adventure. 2. Treat every new assignment as a turnaround, even if it isn't. 3. Question the status quo. 4. Go out and find something that is broken. 5. Add adventure to every job. 6. Break free of routine. 7. Make the adventure fun.

23. John D. Beck and Neil M. Yeager, *The Leader's Window: Mastering the Four Styles of Leadership to Build High Performance Teams* (New York: John Wiley, 1994).

24. See John P. Kotter, *A Force for Change: How Leadership Differs from Management* (New York: The Free Press, 1996), 5.

25. Jay A. Conger, *Learning to Lead : The Art of Transforming Managers into Leaders* (San Francisco: Jossey-Bass, 1992), 92–93. Conger is commenting on material from Kouzes and Posner.

26. Warren G. Bennis, *On Becoming a Leader* (Cambridge, MA: Perseus, 2003), 51.

27. Michael Carey, "Transformational Leadership and the Fundamental Option for Self-Transcendence," *Leadership Quarterly* 3 (1992): 227.

28. Carey, "Transformational Leadership," 227.

29. Harrison Owen, *The Spirit of Leadership* (San Francisco: Berrett-Koehler, 1999), 58.

30. Marcic, *Managing with the Wisdom of Love*, 130.

31. See Henry P. Sims and Peter Lorenzi, *The New Leadership Paradigm* (Newbury, CA: Sage Publications, 1992), 298, where the authors give a table of the fundamentals needed to become a superleader.

32. Gardner, *On Leadership*, xii.

33. Kouzes and Posner, *Credibility*, 19.

34. See Morse, *The Relationship of Wisdom*, 27.

35. David A. Ramey, *Empowering Leaders* (Kansas City, MO: Sheed and Ward, 1991), 216.

36. Bolman and Deal, *Leading with Soul*, 12.

Chapter 3

1. Jack Hawley, *Reawakening the Spirit in Work* (San Francisco: Berrett-Koehlev, 1993), 11.

2. Gardner, *On Leadership*, 132.

3. Kouzes and Posner, *Credibility*, 7.

4. Charles C. Manz and Henry P. Sims, *Superleadership: Leading Others to Lead Themselves* (New York: Prentice Hall, 1984), 53.

5. Kouzes and Posner, *Credibility*, 185.

6. Joe Batten, "Servant Leadership: A Passion to Serve," in *Insights on Leadership*, ed. Larry C. Spears (New York: Wiley, 1994), 41.

7. Kouzes and Posner, *The Leadership Challenge*, xvii.

8. Kouzes and Posner, *The Leadership Challenge*, 239.

9. Koestenbaum, *Leadership: The Inner Side of Greatness*, 50.

10. Koestenbaum, *Leadership: The Inner Side of Greatness*, 17.

11. Gilbert W. Fairholm, *Capturing the Heart of Leadership: Spirituality and Community in the New American Workplace* (Westport, CT: Praeger, 1997), 26.

12. Thomas A Bausch, "Servant-Leaders Making Human Models of Work and Organization," in *Insights on Leadership*, ed. Larry C. Spears (New York: Wiley, 1998), 231.

13. See Paul Chaffee, *Accountable Leadership* (San Francisco: Jossey-Bass, 1997), 11, where the author gives nine standards for accountable leaders.

14. See Manske, *Secrets of Effective Leadership*, 51–58.

15. See Ted W. Engstrom, *The Making of a Christian Leader* (Grand Rapids: Zondervan, 1976), where the author gives a list of these skills.

16. Manz and Sims, *Superleadership*, 7.

17. See Manz and Sims, *Superleadership*, 53.

18. See Kouzes and Posner, *The Leadership Challenge*, 201.

19. Koestenbaum, *Leadership: The Inner Side of Greatness*, 91.

20. John of the Cross, *Spiritual Canticle*, vs. 19.

21. Beck and Yeager, *The Leader's Window*, 7.

22. Max Depree, *Leadership Is an Art* (New York: Doubleday, 1989), 9.

23. See Engstrom, *The Making of a Christian Leader*, 129–30, where he gives seventeen suggestions for how a manager can show concern and

sensitivity for followers, as well as p. 128, where he gives a series of warnings regarding inauthentic approaches to motivation.

24. Kouzes and Posner, *Credibility*, 25.

25. Sims and Lorenzi, *The New Leadership Paradigm*, 79.

26. Leland Kaiser, *The Road Ahead: Transform Yourself, Your Organization, and Your Community* (Englewood, CO: Estes Park Institute, Notes, 1998), 28.

27. Kouzes and Posner, *Credibility*, 31.

28. See Bryman, *Charisma*, 175.

29. See Manz and Sims, *Superleadership*, 222.

30. See Jean Lipman-Blumen, *Connective Leadership* (Oxford: University Press, 1996), 286–324: chapter 11, "Women Leaders."

31. Vennessa V. Druskat, "Gender and Leadership Style: Transformational and Transactional Leadership in the Roman Catholic Church," *Leadership Quarterly* 5 (1994): 101.

32. See Kouzes and Posner, *Credibility*, 157.

33. Gardner, *On Leadership*, 23.

34. See Manz and Sims, *Superleadership*, 43.

35. See McLean and Weitzel, *Leadership: Magic, Myth, or Method*, 86.

36. See Kouzes and Posner, *Credibility*, 3.

37. See Gilbert W. Fairholm, *Mastering Inner Leadership* (Westport, CT: Quorum Books, 2001). For Fairholm "inner leadership" is spiritual leadership, but it also refers to those in the middle of an organization. These are not top leaders but they are leaders nonetheless.

38. Kouzes and Posner, *The Leadership Challenge*, xvii.

39. See Kouzes and Posner, *The Leadership Challenge*, 195.

40. See Kouzes and Posner, *The Leadership Challenge*, 179–85.

41. James A. Belasco and Ralph C. Stayer, *Flight of the Buffalo: Soaring to Excellence, Learning to Let Employees Lead* (New York: Warner Books, 1993), 62.

42. See Kouzes and Posner, *The Leadership Challenge*, 271–75.

43. Stephen R. Covey, "Servant-Leadership from the Inside Out," in *Insights on Leadership*, ed. Larry C. Spears (New York: Wiley, 1998), xvi.

Chapter 4

1. Kouzes and Posner, *The Leadership Challenge*, 30.

2. See Charles Handy and Warren Bennis, *The Age of Unreason* (Boston: Harvard Business School Press, 1990), 231: "Mentoring is a skill on its own. Quiet people have it more than loud people, for mentors are able to live vicariously, getting pleasure from the success of others; they

are interpreters not theorists, nor action people, best perhaps in the reflective stage of learning, people who are attracted by influence not power."

3. See Jaffe and others, *Rekindling Commitment,* 168.

4. For an examination of your own approach to change, see James Cribbin, *Leadership, Your Competitive Edge* (New York: American Management Association, 1981), 201–5; for ten ways to avoid disaster during times of change, see Bennis, *An Invented Life: Reflections on Leadership and Change* (Reading, MA: Addison-Wesley Publishing Co., 1993), 169–71.

5. Handy and Bennis, *The Age of Unreason,* 24.

6. Wilson and others, *Leadership Trapeze,* 12.

7. Jaffe and others, *Rekindling Commitment,* 165.

8. Marcic, *Managing with the Wisdom of Love,* 39—a table that summarizes her insights on these issues.

9. Bennis, *An Invented Life,* 169–71, presents ten ways to avoid disaster during periods of change.

10. See Cribbin, *Leadership, Your Competitive Edge,* 201–5, where the author gives a self-evaluation for leaders on planning for change, diffusing opposition to change, and making the change effective.

11. Two simple descriptions: Jaffe, *Rekindling Commitment,* 149: "A vision has several specific qualities: 1. It motivates and inspires. 2. It is a 'stretch,' it pushes people toward greatness. 3. It is clear and concrete. 4. It is achievable. 5. It reflects the company's highest values. 6. It is simple, clear and easy to communicate." Burt Nanus, "Vision: The Key to Leadership," in *Visionary Leadership* (San Francisco: Jossey-Bass Publishers, 1992), 16: "The right vision attracts commitment and energizes people. The right vision creates meaning in workers' lives. The right vision establishes a standard of excellence. The right vision bridges the present and future."

12. See Cronin, "Thinking and Learning about Leadership," 23.

13. Nanus, "Vision: The Key to Leadership," 19–20.

14. See A. Manasse, "Vision and Leadership: Paying Attention to Intention," *Peabody Journal of Education* 63 (Fall 1986): 150–73.

15. Koestenbaum, *Leadership: The Inner Side of Greatness,* 84.

16. Nanus, *Visionary Leadership,* 19–20, gives eight warning signs that an organization needs a new vision.

17. See Nanus, *Visionary Leadership,* 16.

18. See Jaffe and others, *Rekindling Commitment,* 152–53.

19. See Conger and Kanugo, *Charismatic Leadership;* for a fine "Communication checklist," see Smith, *The New Leader,* 127–28.

20. See Mary McFarland, *The Process of Vision Development Described by Six College and University Presidents* (Spokane: Gonzaga University Doctoral

Dissertation, 1993), 107, where the author lists seven vision command-ments articulated by the presidents she interviewed. 1. Reflect on per-sonal values as they will influence the vision, 2. Scan the environment while exploring the parameters of the vision, 3. Ask questions and then listen to many diverse voices including ideas of those with dissimilar views, 4. Stay fresh in thought by reading and reflecting, 5. Allow the vision to be transformed by others—for in the end the vision belongs to the insti-tution, 6. Pursue the vision with passion so it may be a driving force on the institutional agenda, and 7. Prepare the institution for the future—but let the work of vision attainment begin as soon as possible.

21. Koestenbaum, *Leadership: The Inner Side of Greatness*, 123.

22. Frank T. Barrett, "Creating Appreciative Learning Cultures," *Organizational Dynamics* 23 (Autumn, 1995): 48.

23. Yair Berson, Boas Shamir, Bruce J. Avolio, and Micha Popper, "The Relationship between Vision and Strength, Leadership Style, and Context," *Leadership Quarterly* 12 (2001): 56.

24. 1. Practice influencing others to be involved in a mission they have never been involved in before. 2. Seek to identify others' contribu-tion to your community's shared vision. 3. Treat everyone with respect, clearly indicating to them that you are convinced they have a lot to con-tribute to your community. 4. Plan a series of deliberate delegations to a specified number of individuals in your community. 5. Provide relational and educational support to each person who responds to your delega-tion. 6. Treat your community as dedicated individuals whose gifts you must channel, not as an amorphous passive group.

25. See Richard O. Wolfe, *Synergy: Increasing Production with People, Ideas, and Things* (Dubuque: Kendall & Hunt, 1993), 4.

26. See Wilson and others, *Leadership Trapeze*, 73–79.

27. Geoffrey M. Bellman, *Getting Things Done When You Are Not in Charge* (San Francisco: Barrett-Koehler, 1992), 21, gives seven criteria to measure whether a person is able to hold on to values.

28. McLean and Weitzel, *Leadership: Magic, Myth, or Method*, 186.

29. See the principles for success in consultation with others, as presented by Marcic, *Managing with the Wisdom of Love*, 107; and the val-ues of the model leader in William D. Hitt, *The Model Leader: A Fully Functioning Person* (Columbus: Battelle, 1993), 97.

30. See Hitt, *The Model Leader*, 107–9, where he gives the following suggestions on coaching: —Take the time to build a personal relationship with each of your staff members; —Give special attention to each staff member at the beginning of a new job assignment; —Use naturally aris-ing interactions with staff to foster learning; —Use work assignments effectively as a primary means of staff development; —Master the art of

delegation; —Give honest feedback on a timely basis; —Use performance appraisal as a means of teaching, not exhorting or punishing; and —Take stock of personal considerations.

31. See Conger, *Learning to Lead,* 44–45.

32. See McLean and Weitzel, *Leadership: Magic, Myth, or Method,* 203, for a few suggestions on examining your own leadership style. 1. What fears are keeping me from stepping forward to lead? (personal risk) 2. What am I giving to life and getting from life? (personal priority) 3. Am I yet wise enough to make a leadership contribution? (personal knowledge) 4. Am I otherwise equipped to accept the responsibility for leading others? (personal abilities).

33. Kouzes and Posner give a list of key practices of exemplary leaders that can be a healthy examination for every leader. See *Leadership Challenge,* 7–14.

34. Kouzes and Posner, *Leadership Challenge,* xvii.

Chapter 5

1. See Kouzes and Posner, *Credibility,* 92.

2. See Edwin P. Hollander, "Leadership, Followership, Self, and Others," *Leadership Quarterly* 3 (1992): 51.

3. Bennis, *On Becoming a Leader,* 51.

4. Conger, *Learning to Lead,* 100.

5. Ramey, *Empowering Leaders,* 67.

6. Stogdill, *Handbook of Leadership,* 52.

7. Senge, *Fifth Discipline,* 8.

8. See Fred Kofman and Peter M. Senge, "Communities of Commitment: The Heart of Learning Organizations," *Organizational Dynamics* 21 (Autumn, 1993): 7.

9. Marcic, *Managing with the Wisdom of Love,* 19.

10. Cribbin, *Leadership, Your Competitive Edge,* 87, gives a series of basic ideas about human interaction that explain what is important to people within an organization.

11. Marcic, *Managing with the Wisdom of Love,* 121–22, gives an excellent list of questions that any individual or group can ask to clarify the level of trust within the organization.

12. James R, Carlopio, "Holism: A Philosophy of Organizational Leadership for the Future," *Leadership Quarterly* 5 (1994): 305.

13. Kouzes and Posner, *Credibility,* 51.

14. Kouzes and Posner, *Credibility,* 9. See also 108–10.

15. Robert W. Terry, *Authentic Leadership: Courage in Action* (San Francisco: Jossey-Bass, 1993), 274.

16. Ramey, *Empowering Leaders,* xiii.

17. Some of the practical "dos" and "don'ts"of such a leader are given by Smith, *The New Leader,* 100–101.

18. Ramey, *Empowering Leaders,* 217.

19. Marcic, *Managing with the Wisdom of Love,* 121–22, gives twelve excellent recommendations which are very practical while constitutive of a vision that results from managing with the wisdom of love.

Chapter 6

1. See Ramey, *Empowering Leaders,* 94.

2. Perhaps we can be challenged by George Bernard Shaw who said: "Few people think more than two or three times a year. I have made an international reputation for myself by thinking once or twice a week."

3. Ritscher, "Spiritual Leadership," 66. See also Kofman and Senge, "Communities of Commitment," 5–23, where the authors insist on page 7 that real leadership learning takes place "in a continuous cycle of theoretical action and practical conceptualization."

4. Kaiser, *The Road Ahead,* 2.

5. Nancy J. Eggert, *Contemplative Leadership for Entrepreneurial Organizations* (Westport, CT: Quorum Books, 1998), 231. See also Marilyn Wood Daudelin, "Learning from Experience through Reflection," *Organizational Dynamics* 24 (Winter, 1996): 36–48.

6. I use the word *prayer* along with other religious terms since leadership is an intimate part of who a person is. For the religious person there can be no separation of the inner self's awareness of God from any aspect of life.

7. Hawley, *Reawakening the Spirit in Work,* viii.

8. Eggert, *Contemplative Leadership,* 123.

9. In this section I suggest components of the nature of contemplation. For Eggert's view, see *Contemplative Leadership,* 114–18.

10. See Koestenbaum, *Leadership: The Inner Side of Greatness,* 131.

11. Koestenbaum, *Leadership: The Inner Side of Greatness,* 123.

12. Koestenbaum, *Leadership: The Inner Side of Greatness,* 93.

13. Pulley, *Losing Your Job—Reclaiming Your Spirit,* 148.

14. Matthew Fox, *The Reinvention of Work* (San Francisco: Harper and Row, 1994), 147.

15. Pulley, *Losing Your Job—Reclaiming Your Spirit,* 207.

16. Kaiser, *The Road Ahead,* 2.

17. Greenleaf, "The Servant as Leader," in *Servant Leadership*, 28.

18. Hitt, *The Model Leader*, 11. See also Bennis, *On Becoming a Leader*, 54–64, for lessons on knowledge.

19. Manske, *Secrets of Effective Leadership*, 92–94, gives twelve excellent and practical approaches and techniques to improve listening skills.

20. Kaiser, *The Road Ahead*, 126.

21. For similar ideas to those developed in this section see my book *Leisure: A Spiritual Need* (Notre Dame, IN: Ave Maria Press, 1990), chapters 5 and 6.

Chapter 7

1. Jaffe and others, *Rekindling Commitment*, 49.

2. Marcic, *Managing with the Wisdom of Love*, 113.

3. Peter Vail, "Process Wisdom for a New Age," in *Transforming Work*, ed. John D. Adams (Alexandria, VA: Miles River Press, 1984), 33, 27, 25.

4. Cribbin, *Leadership, Your Competitive Edge*, 61–78, presents a very good collection of self-given evaluations and questionnaires on analyzing your organization.

5. See Ritscher, "Spiritual Leadership," 62, where he gives ten new leadership skills needed to manage the spirit of an organization.

6. See Graham, "Servant-Leadership in Organizations: Inspirational and Moral," 106, where she comments on the impact on followers of this kind of leadership.

7. See Sims and Lorenzi, *The New Leadership Paradigm*, 170.

8. See Gardner, *On Leadership*, 22.

9. Alan W. Randolph, "Navigating the Journey to Empowerment," *Organizational Dynamics* 23 (Spring, 1995): 30.

10. See Cribbin, *Leadership, Your Competitive Edge*, 6–8.

11. See Marsha Sinetar, "Entrepreneurs, Chaos and Creativity: Can Creative People Survive Large Company Structure?" in *Frontiers of Leadership*, ed. Michel Syrett and Clare Hogg (Oxford, UK: Blackwell Publishers, 1992), 115.

12. Comments of Dr. Joe Albert, "Motivating the Spirit at Work: Bridging the Gap between Quality and Motivation," Gonzaga University, February 22, 2001.

13. See Randolph, "Navigating the Journey to Empowerment," 28.

14. See Manz and Sims, *Superleadership*, 201–2, where the authors give leader behaviors for self-managed teams.

15. See Wilson and others, *The Leadership Trapeze*, 115–16.

16. See Loughlan Sofield and Carroll Juliano, *Collaborative Ministry* (Notre Dame, IN: Ave Maria Press, 1987), 19, 22.

17. Terry, *Authentic Leadership*, 40.

18. See Sims and Lorenzi, *New leadership Paradigm*, 42–43, where they speak about organizational citizenship behaviors (OCBs) and give altruism, courtesy, sportsmanship, civic virtue, and conscientiousness as qualities that enrich the organization's growth and solidarity.

19. Markham, *Spiritlinking*, 2–3.

20. For a different approach to organizational cycles, see Jaffe and others, *Rekindling Commitment*, 104, and Cribbin, *Leadership, Your Competitive Edge*, 49.

21. Jaffe and others, *Rekindling Commitment*, 138–39.

22. Jaffe and others, *Rekindling Commitment*, 149.

23. See the web page, ethics.iit.edu/codes.

24. See Leonard Doohan, *Grass Roots Pastors* (San Francisco: Harper and Row, 1989), 16, where I also refer to stages in conflict management suggested by Thomas Sweetser and Carol Wisniewski.

25. Kaiser, *The Road Ahead*, 14.

Chapter 8

1. E. Kurtz and K. Ketcham, *Spirituality of Imperfection: Modern Wisdom from Classic Stories* (New York: Bantam, 1992), 35.

2. See Marcic, *Managing with the Wisdom of Love*, 126–27.

3. Pulley, *Losing Your Job—Reclaiming Your Spirit*, 158.

4. See Karl Rahner, *The Practice of Faith*, ed. Karl Lehmann and Albert Raffelt (New York: Crossroad, 1984), 18–26.

5. See Leonard Doohan, *The Lay-Centered Church* (San Francisco: Harper and Row, 1984), 103–19.

6. See Rahner, *The Practice of Faith*, 22.

7. Lillian Thomas Shank, "Ordinary Mysticism and Ordinary Mystics," *Way* 30 (1990): 231.

8. Matthew Fox, *A Spirituality Named Compassion* (Minneapolis: Winston Press, 1979), iii.

9. Bernard Mullahy, *The Splendid Risk* (Notre Dame, IN: University of Notre Dame Press, 1982), 29.

10. Richard J. Hauser, *Moving in the Spirit* (New York/Mahwah, NJ: Paulist Press, 1986), 5.

11. Rahner, *The Practice of Faith*, 21–22.

12. Matthew Fox, *Coming of the Cosmic Christ* (San Francisco: Harper and Row, 1988), 185.

13. Mullahy, *The Splendid Risk*, 149.

Conclusion

1. See Kotter, *A Force for Change*, 139.

2. Kotter, *A Force for Change*, 126.

3. See John Kotter, *The Leadership Factor* (New York: The Free Press, 1988), 94.

4. Marcic, *Managing with the Wisdom of Love*, 39.

5. See Carey, "Transformational Leadership," 220, and "Transformative Christian Leadership," 31.

6. See Yeon Choi and Renate R. Mai-Dalton, "The Model of Followers' Responses to Self-Sacrificial Leadership: An Empirical Test," *Leadership Quarterly* 10 (1999): 397–421.

7. Jim Collins comments: "Executives must accept the fact that the exercise of true leadership is inversely proportional to the exercise of power." "And the Walls Came Tumbling Down," in *Leading beyond the Walls*, ed. Hesselbein and others, 25.

8. Bernard Bass, "From Transactional to Transformational Leadership: Learning to Share the Vision," *Organizational Dynamics* 18 (1990): 21.

9. Jaffe and others, *Rekindling Commitment*, 18.

10. Smith, *The New Leader*, 178.

11. See Arthur Shriberg, Carol Lloyd, David L. Shriberg, and Mary Lynn Williamson, *Practicing Leadership* (New York: John Wiley, 1997), 80: effective listening, and 83: effective feedback.

12. See Sims and Lorenzi, *The New Leadership Paradigm*, 104, for comments on effective organizational rewards and disincentives.

13. For some good tips on effective goal setting, see Sims and Lorenzi, *The New Leadership Paradigm*, 134.

14. Barrett, "Creating Appreciative Learning Cultures," 39–40.

15. See, for example, Chanoch Jacobsen and Robert J. House, "Dynamics of Charismatic Leadership: A Process Theory, Simulation Model and Tests," *Leadership Quarterly* 12 (2001): 75–112.

16. James G. Hunt, "Transformational/Charismatic Leadership's Transformation of the Field: An Historical Essay," *Leadership Quarterly* 10 (1999): 140.

17. Batten, "Servant Leadership," 38.

18. Markham, *Spiritlinking*, 6.

19. Nanus, "Vision: The Key to Leadership," 3.

20. Ritscher, "Spiritual Leadership," 6.

BIBLIOGRAPHY

Adams, John D., ed. *Transforming Work*. Alexandria, VA: Miles River Press, 1984.

Badaracco, Joseph. *Leadership and the Quest for Integrity*. Boston, MA: Harvard Business School Press, 1989.

Barrett, Frank T. "Creating Appreciative Learning Cultures." *Organizational Dynamics* 23 (Autumn, 1995): 39–48.

Bass, Bernard. "From Transactional to Transformational Leadership: Learning to Share the Vision." *Organizational Dynamics* 18 (1990): 19–36.

Batten, Joe. "Servant Leadership: A Passion to Serve." In *Insights on Leadership*, ed. Larry C. Spears, 38–53. New York: Wiley, 1998.

Bausch, Thomas A. "Servant-Leaders Making Human Models of Work and Organization." In *Insights on Leadership*, ed. Larry C. Spears, 230–45. New York: Wiley, 1998.

Beck, John D., and Neil M. Yeager. *The Leader's Window: Mastering the Four Styles of Leadership to Build High Performance Teams*. New York: John Wiley, 1994.

Belasco, James A., and Ralph C. Stayer. *Flight of the Buffalo: Soaring to Excellence, Learning to Let Employees Lead*. New York: Warner Books, 1993.

Bellman, Geoffrey M. *Getting Things Done When You Are Not in Charge*. San Francisco: Barrett-Koehler, 1992.

Bennis, Warren G. *An Invented Life: Reflections on Leadership and Change*. New York: Basic Books, 1994.

———. *On Becoming a Leader*. Cambridge, MA: Perseus, 2003.

———. "Transformative Power and Leadership." In *Leadership and Organizational Culture*, ed. T. J. Sergiovanni and J. E. Corbally, 64–67. Urbana: University of Illinois Press, 1984.

Bennis, Warren G., and B. Nanus. *Leaders: The Strategies for Taking Charge*. New York: Harper and Row, 1985.

Berson, Yair, Boas Shamir, Bruce J. Avolio, and Micha Popper. "The Relationship between Vision and Strength, Leadership Style, and Context." *Leadership Quarterly* 12 (2001): 53–73.

Black, Warren. *The 9 Natural Laws of Leadership.* New York: AMACOM, 1995.

Bolman, Lee G., and Terrence E. Deal. *Leading with Soul: An Uncommon Journey of Spirit.* San Francisco: Jossey-Bass, 1995.

Bryman, Alan. *Charisma and Leadership in Organizations.* London: Sage Publications, 1992.

———. *Leadership and Organizations.* London: Routledge and Kegan Paul, 1986.

Burns, James MacGregor. *Leadership.* New York: Harper and Row, 1978.

Callahan, Kennon L. *Effective Church Leadership.* San Francisco: Harper and Row, 1990.

Carey, Michael. "Transformational Leadership and the Fundamental Option for Self-Transcendence." *Leadership Quarterly* 3 (1992): 217–36.

———. "Transformative Christian Leadership." *Human Development* 12 (1991): 30–34.

Carlopio, James R. "Holism: A Philosophy of Organizational Leadership for the Future." *Leadership Quarterly* 5 (1994): 297–307.

Cashman, Kevin. *Leadership from the Inside Out.* Provo, UT: Executive Excellence Publishing, 1998.

Chaffee, Paul. *Accountable Leadership.* San Francisco: Jossey-Bass, 1997.

Choi, Yeon, and Renate R. Mai-Dalton. "The Model of Followers' Responses to Self-Sacrificial Leadership: An Empirical Test." *Leadership Quarterly* 10 (1999): 397–421.

Collins, Jim. "And the Walls Came Tumbling Down." In *Leading beyond the Walls,* ed. Frances Hesselbein, Marshall Goldsmith, and Ian Somerville, 19–28. San Francisco: Jossey-Bass, 1999.

Conger, Jay A. *Learning to Lead: The Art of Transforming Managers into Leaders.* San Francisco: Jossey-Bass, 1992.

———. *Spirit at Work: Discovering the Spirituality in Leadership.* San Francisco: Jossey-Bass, 1994.

Conger, Jay A., and Rabinda N. Kanugo. *Charismatic Leadership: The Elusive Factor in Organizational Effectiveness.* San Francisco: Jossey-Bass, 1988.

Covey, Stephen R. *Principle-centered Leadership.* New York: Simon and Schuster, 1991.

———. "Servant-Leadership from the Inside Out." In *Insights on Leadership,* ed. Larry C. Spears, xi–xviii. New York: Wiley, 1998.

Cox, Charles J., and Cary L. Cooper. "Characteristics of the Successful Chief Executive." In *Frontiers of Leadership,* ed. Michel Syrett and Clare Hogg, 79–82. Oxford: Blackwell Publishers, 1992.

Cribbin, James. *Leadership, Your Competitive Edge.* New York: American Management Association, 1981.

Cronin, Thomas E. "Thinking and Learning about Leadership." In *Contemporary Issues in Leadership,* ed. William E. Rosenbach and Robert L. Taylor, 45–64. San Francisco: Westview Press, 1993.

Depree, Max. *Leadership Is an Art.* New York: Doubleday, 1989.

Doohan, Leonard. *Grass Roots Pastors.* San Francisco: Harper and Row, 1989.

———. *The Lay-Centered Church.* San Francisco: Harper and Row, 1984.

Druskat, Vennessa V. "Gender and Leadership Style: Transformational and Transactional Leadership in the Roman Catholic Church." *Leadership Quarterly* 5 (1994): 99–119.

Eggert, Nancy J. *Contemplative Leadership for Entrepreneurial Organizations.* Westport, CT: Quorum Books, 1998.

Engstrom, Ted W. *The Making of a Christian Leader.* Grand Rapids: Zondervan, 1976.

Fairholm, Gilbert W. *Capturing the Heart of Leadership: Spirituality and Community in the New American Workplace.* Westport, CT: Praeger, 1997.

———. *Mastering Inner Leadership.* Westport, CT: Quorum Books, 2001.

———. *The Techniques of Inner Leadership.* Westport, CT: Praeger, 2003.

Fox, Matthew. *Coming of the Cosmic Christ.* San Francisco: Harper and Row, 1988.

———. *The Reinvention of Work.* San Francisco: Harper and Row, 1994.

———. *A Spirituality Named Compassion.* Minneapolis: Winston Press, 1979.

Gardner, John. *On Leadership.* New York: The Free Press, 1990.

Graham, Jill W. "Servant-Leadership in Organizations: Inspirational and Moral." *Leadership Quarterly* 2 (1991): 113.

Greenleaf, Robert K. *The Power of Servant Leadership.* Edited by Larry C. Spears. San Francisco: Berrett-Koehler, 1998.

———. *Servant Leadership: A Journey into the Nature of Legitimate Power and Greatness.* New York: Paulist Press, 1977.

———. *The Servant Leader Within.* Edited by Hamilton Beazley, Julie Beggs, and Larry C Spears. New York/Mahwah, NJ: Paulist Press, 2003.

Grint, Keith. *The Arts of Leadership.* Oxford: Oxford University Press, 2000.

Hallstein, Richard. *Memoirs of a Recovering Autocrat.* San Francisco: Barrett-Koehler, 1992.

Handy, Charles, and Warren Bennis. *The Age of Unreason*. Boston: Harvard Business School Press, 1990.

Hauser, Richard J. *Moving in the Spirit*. New York: Paulist Press, 1986.

Hawley, Jack. *Reawakening the Spirit in Work*. San Francisco: Berrett-Koehler Publishers, 1993.

Hesselbein, Frances, Marshall Goldsmith, and Ian Somerville, eds. *Leading beyond the Walls*. San Francisco: Jossey-Bass, 1999.

Hitt, William D. *The Model Leader: A Fully Functioning Person*. Columbus, OH: Battelle Press, 1993.

Hollander, Edwin P. "Leadership, Followership, Self, and Others." *Leadership Quarterly* 3 (1992): 43–54.

Hosmer, LaRue T. *Moral Leadership in Business*. Burr Ridge, IL: Irwin, 1994.

Hunt, James G. "Transformational/Charismatic Leadership's Transformation of the Field: An Historical Essay." *Leadership Quarterly* 10 (1999): 129–44.

Jacobsen, Chanoch, and Robert J. House. "Dynamics of Charismatic Leadership: A Process Theory, Simulation Model and Tests." *Leadership Quarterly* 12 (2001): 75–112.

Jaffe, Dennis T., Cynthia D. Scott, and Glenn R. Tobe. *Rekindling Commitment*. San Francisco: Jossey-Bass, 1994.

Kaiser, Leland. *The Road Ahead: Transform Yourself, Your Organization, and Your Community*. Englewood, CO: Estes Park Institute, Notes, 1998.

Kidder, Rushworth M. *Shared Values for a Troubled World*. San Francisco: Jossey-Bass, 1994.

Koestenbaum, Peter. *Leadership: The Inner Side of Greatness*. San Francisco: Jossey-Bass, 1991.

Kofman, Fred, and Peter M. Senge. "Communities of Commitment: The Heart of Learning Organizations." *Organizational Dynamics* 21 (Autumn, 1993): 5–23.

Kotter, John P. *A Force for Change: How Leadership Differs from Management*. New York: The Free Press, 1996.

———. *The Leadership Factor*. New York: The Free Press, 1988.

———. *What Leaders Really Do*. Boston: Harvard Business School Press, 1999.

Kouzes, J. M., and B. Z. Posner. *Credibility: How Leaders Gain and Lose It, Why People Demand It*. San Francisco: Jossey-Bass, 1993.

———. *The Leadership Challenge: How to Get Extraordinary Things Done in Organizations*. San Francisco: Jossey-Bass, 1988.

Kurtz, E., and K. Ketcham. *Spirituality of Imperfection: Modern Wisdom from Classic Stories*. New York: Bantam, 1992.

Laborde, Genie. *Influencing with Integrity*. Palo Alto, CA: Science and Behavior Books, Syntony Publ. Co., 1983.

Lipman-Blumen, Jean. *Connective Leadership.* Oxford: Oxford University Press, 1996.

Manasse, A. "Vision and Leadership: Paying Attention to Intention." *Peabody Journal of Education* 63 (Fall, 1986): 150–73.

Manske, Fred A. *The Secrets of Effective Leadership.* Germantown, TN: Leadership Education and Development, 1987.

Manz, Charles C., and Henry P. Sims. *Superleadership: Leading Others to Lead Themselves.* New York: Prentice Hall, 1984.

Marcic, Dorothy. *Managing with the Wisdom of Love.* San Francisco: Jossey-Bass, 1995.

Markham, Donna J. *Spiritlinking Leadership.* New York: Paulist Press, 1999.

Maskoff, Barbara, and Gary Wenet. *The Inner Work of Leaders: Leadership as a Habit of Mind.* New York: AMACOM, 2000.

McFarland, Mary. *The Process of Vision Development Described by Six College and University Presidents.* Spokane, WA: Gonzaga University, Doctoral Dissertation, 1993.

McLean, J. W., and William Weitzel. *Leadership: Magic, Myth, or Method.* New York: AMACOM, 1992.

Morse, Mary Kate. *The Relationship of Wisdom to Transformational Leadership.* Spokane, WA: Gonzaga University, Doctoral Dissertation, 1996.

Moxley, Russ. *Leadership and Spirit.* San Francisco: Jossey-Bass, 2000.

Mullahy, Bernard. *The Splendid Risk.* Notre Dame, IN: University of Notre Dame Press, 1982.

Nanus, Burt. "Vision: The Key to Leadership." In *Visionary Leadership.* San Francisco: Jossey-Bass Publishers, 1992.

Owen, Harrison. *The Spirit of Leadership.* San Francisco: Berrett-Koehler, 1999.

Palmer, Parker J. Foreword. In *Seeker and Servant: The Private Writings of Robert K. Greenleaf,* ed. Anne T. Fraker and Larry C. Spears, xi–xii. San Francisco: Jossey-Bass, 1996.

Pulley, Mary L. *Losing Your Job—Reclaiming Your Spirit.* San Francisco: Jossey-Bass, 1997.

Rahner, Karl. *Practice of Faith.* Edited by Karl Lehmann and Albert Raffelt. New York: Crossroad, 1984.

Ramey, David A. *Empowering Leaders.* Kansas City, MO: Sheed and Ward, 1991.

Randolph, Alan W. "Navigating the Journey to Empowerment." *Organizational Dynamics* 23 (Spring, 1995): 19–32.

Ritscher, James A. "Spiritual Leadership." In *Transforming Leadership: From Vision to Results*, ed. John D. Adams, 61–80. Alexandria, VA: Miles River Press, 1986.

Sankowsky, Daniel. "The Charismatic Leader as Narcissist: Understanding the Abuse of Power." *Organizational Dynamics* 23 (Spring, 1995): 57–71.

Senge, Peter. *The Fifth Discipline: The Art and Practice of the Learning Organization.* New York: Doubleday, 1990.

———. "Leadership in Living Organizations." In *Leading beyond the Walls*, ed. F. Hesselbein and others, 73–90. San Francisco: Jossey-Bass, 1999.

Shank, Lillian Thomas. "Ordinary Mysticism and Ordinary Mystics." *Way* 30 (1990): 231–44.

Shriberg, Arthur, Carol Lloyd, David L. Shriberg, and Mary Lynn Williamson. *Practicing Leadership.* New York: John Wiley, 1997.

Sims, Henry P., and Peter Lorenzi. *The New Leadership Paradigm.* Newbury, CA: Sage Publications, 1992.

Sinetar, Marsha. "Entrepreneurs, Chaos and Creativity: Can Creative People Survive Large Company Structure?" In *Frontiers of Leadership*, ed. Michel Syrett and Clare Hogg, 109–16. Oxford, UK: Blackwell Publishers, 1992.

Smith, Gregory P. *The New Leader: Bringing Creativity and Innovation to the Workplace.* Delray Beach, FL: St. Lucie Press, 1997.

Sofield, Loughlan, and Carroll Juliano. *Collaborative Ministry.* Notre Dame, IN: Ave Maria Press, 1987.

Spears, Larry C., ed. *Insights on Leadership.* New York: Wiley, 1998.

Spitzer, Robert J. *The Spirit of Leadership.* Provo, UT: Executive Excellence Publishing, 2000.

Stogdill, Ralph M. *Handbook of Leadership.* New York: The Free Press, 1974.

Syrett, Michel, and Clare Hogg, eds. "Take Me to Your Leader." In *Frontiers of Leadership: An Essential Reader.* Oxford: Blackwell Publishers, 1992.

Terry, Robert W. *Authentic Leadership: Courage in Action.* San Francisco: Jossey-Bass, 1993.

Tichy, Noel M., and Mary Anne Devanna. *The Transformational Leader.* New York: Wiley, 1986.

Vail, Peter. "Process Wisdom for a New Age." In *Transforming Work*, ed. John D. Adams, 18–34. Alexandria, VA: Miles River Press, 1984.

Wilson, Jeanne M., Jill George, Richard S. Wellins, and William C. Byham. *Leadership Trapeze.* San Francisco: Jossey-Bass, 1994.

Wolfe, Richard O. *Synergy: Increasing Production with People, Ideas, and Things.* Dubuque: Kendall & Hunt, 1993.
Wood Daudelin, Marilyn. "Learning from Experience through Reflection." *Organizational Dynamics* 24 (Winter, 1996): 36–48.

INITIATIVE